LEAD WITH THE LEFT

Manny Shinwell

LEAD WITH THE LEFT

My First Ninety-six Years

CASSELL
LONDON

CASSELL LTD.
35 Red Lion Square, London WC1R 4SG
and at Sydney, Auckland, Toronto, Johannesburg,
an affiliate of
Macmillan Publishing Co., Inc.,
New York.

First published 1981

ISBN 0 304 30497 2

Typeset by Inforum Ltd.
Portsmouth
Printed in the U.S.A.

To my daughters Lucy and Rose

CONTENTS

ILLUSTRATIONS

ACKNOWLEDGEMENTS AND CONFESSIONS

Opinions and references to significant political events expressed are my exclusive responsibility. The exceptions are a commentary by Bill Connor, brilliant columnist of the *Daily Mirror* — regrettably no longer with us — on my behaviour between 1964 and 1967 as Chairman of the Parliamentary Labour Party and on my subsequent resignation, for which permission to quote was readily granted; the article on my lifestyle when transferred from the House of Commons to the House of Lords, reproduced by permission of the magazine *Vogue*; and the extract quoted from *Your Voice* by courtesy of Cicely Berry, the author of this excellent book on elocution, who interviewed me on my method of speaking without notes.

My thanks are also due to a senior librarian of the House of Lords who relieved my anxiety when searching for accurate dates and references in our Parliamentary Reports, advising me where in our vast library the information was available.

I must, however, confess to several omissions. In a book of average size this is inevitable; references to childhood and adolescence hardly matter, and to recount the varied experiences of almost seventy-five years of public life in the absence of a diary (I have never kept one) was in itself a daunting challenge.

Above all, I express gratitude to the publishers for their diplomatic skill, and to their editor, Mr Harry Miller, who, after meticulous scrutiny, suggested emendations, brushing out literary imperfections, causing no personal offence. Wholehearted gratitude is also due to my shorthand writer, Dorothy Golding, who, for a period of over twelve months, endured my intermittent dictation. Surely, together they make a combination worthy of success.

1

East End Childhood

The purpose of this book is not to gain public applause or the approval of Parliamentary colleagues; more likely it could have the contrary effect for the contents are mostly about myself. Should this self-portrait seem to indicate egotism or vanity, or a combination of both, let me say that it arose from a proposal by some friends, endorsed by a publisher, that the time had arrived to reveal my origins, varied environment, political and social behaviour including persistent intervention in local, national and international affairs — and conceal nothing.

Looking back over events, significant and otherwise, plus many disagreeable episodes, and frequent subjection to harsh criticism — to which I have responded in characteristic fashion — I take as my starting-point an appropriate quotation from the Book of Job, chapter 5, verse 7. 'Man is born unto trouble as the sparks fly upward.'

I lived in Glasgow for over thirty years, engaging in various activities, gaining some prominence — some might say notoriety — and also acquiring a Scottish accent. Frequently, people hearing me speak say, 'You're a Scot, are ye not?' Though flattered at the distinction, I am not a native of Scotland. The fact is that I was born in London. How do I know the details? Well, some months ago I was informed by a prominent citizen of London that I was to become a Freeman of the City. Custom required the production of my birth certificate but, despite extensive search, it could not be found, so I obtained a copy. Thus, at a cost of six pounds, I learned to my astonishment that my birthplace was number 17 Freeman Street, in Spitalfields on the fringe of the City of London; the date 18 October 1884.

My father's name, as given on the birth certificate, was Samuel Shinewell. Some years later I learned that at the end of

1

the Boer War, in the early 1900s, my paternal grandfather and my father's younger brother Harry, when emigrating to South Africa, made a slight change in the name by deleting an 'e'; thus the name became Shinwell and so it has remained ever since. My mother's name as shown on the certificate was Rose Koeningswinter, which was the name of a German town. People often adopted the name of a place as their own. Many families had escaped from persecution in Spain and Portugal to Germany, and my mother's people had then gone to Holland and eventually come to England, where they became part of the Dutch community.

I was delighted with the honour of Freeman of the City of London. There was an impressive ceremony and an excellent lunch attended by a number of people associated with the City Corporation. The street of my birth, so I learned, was not the reason for the honour. That was unknown at the time to my sponsors and even to myself; my birth certificate was lost when I was a child and I had never troubled to renew it. Those who initiated the idea had heard me speak at a function and, though my political views were unacceptable, admired my patriotic sentiments. They were kind enough to say they liked my style of speech.

This event, naturally, evokes memories of my early environment. Spitalfields was a district inhabited almost exclusively by immigrants who had left Amsterdam and Rotterdam in the '50s of the last century. It was not an imposed ghetto but a self-contained colony consisting of a few narrow densely populated streets with small and squalid dwellings. The overcrowding and lack of sanitation made the whole area unhygienic, but the local authority regarded this as normal and inevitable. Trade recession caused vast unemployment, which was largely responsible for the great dock strike of 1889, when dockers who were only occasionally employed were demanding a basic wage of sixpence an hour. My father was also unemployed, failing to obtain suitable work in London and, because of our precarious existence, compelled to seek employment in places like Leeds, Manchester and Glasgow. One incident sticks in my memory. My father was about to leave London again and there was opposition from my mother which led to some shouting and language which I was too young to understand. I clung to her skirts and cried my eyes out.

During my father's absence my mother obtained employment as a cook in one of the schools sponsored by a charitable organisation where breakfasts were provided free of charge to the children of poor parents. One winter morning she dressed me as warmly as I suppose her circumstances allowed, then led me through dismal streets with gaslights flickering — there was no electric lighting in those days — to the school. When other children arrived, the breakfast was almost ready. It consisted of porridge with no milk, and coffee. This continued for a couple of months until my father, again out of work, returned to London. He was furious when he discovered that my mother had taken a job. It had apparently not occurred to him that the trifling amount he managed to send home failed to pay even the rent. In those days working-class husbands felt humiliated when their wives went out to work. Unable to pay the rent, we went to live with my maternal grandparents in their house of four tiny rooms, two up and two down. We had one room. Several of my relatives, uncles, aunts and adult cousins, lived in the neighbourhood. Most of the men were employed in diamond cutting, diamond polishing or cigar making. The diamond cutters were the aristocrats of the industry, usually working at home, and occasionally earning good money. The diamond polishers and cigar makers were not so well off.

During periods of recession some of the younger men were fortunate to obtain even casual work at the London Docks. One of my aunts had married a docker. He was a hefty, tough-looking customer, unable to read or write — at that time quite usual among dockers. Because he worked at the docks he was for me a romantic character: working among ships seemed much more interesting than cutting diamonds or working in the clothing trade as my father did. Years later when I was invited to address meetings in London, he was always present and insisted on acting as my bodyguard; not that I needed protection, but it seemed to please him.

My docker uncle was a native of Portugal. The marriage was not regarded with favour by the family. The Dutch preferred to integrate only with the Dutch. Those who had come from other countries, like the Poles, kept to themselves in other parts of the East End and frowned on marriage with any of Dutch or

Russian origin. When my father, whose parents had escaped from persecution in Poland in the early '60s of the last century, married my mother, it caused a sensation in the family. My paternal grandfather, who was a Master Baker in Leeds, and strictly orthodox in religion, regarded marriage with a Dutch person as almost a mortal sin.

The Dutch were believed to hold liberal views about Judaism. The term 'liberal' has no political connotation in this connection. Although the Dutch adhered to the Five Books of Moses they failed occasionally to practise every line of the civil and canonical law of the Pentateuch, either as respecting ritual or food. They were not strictly orthodox by comparison with the ultra orthodoxy and strict observance of Judaism of my paternal grandfather, whose literal conception of Jewish law, known as the Torah, was the cause of friction between himself and many of his Jewish neighbours. For example, he would not attend, either on the Sabbath day or on the principal feasts, that is, the Jewish New Year and Yom Kippur (the Day of Atonement), at the usual synagogue, but gathered a small congregation of friends who were in agreement with his views, in his large bakehouse in Bridge Street, Leeds, where he conducted the service. As a member of the priestly tribe of Levi he was permitted to conduct the prayers.

My researches, admittedly limited, have disclosed no more than that my paternal grandfather and members of his family were flour millers in the northern part of Poland, known as Kovno Guberniya, and emigrated to England about the year 1863 provoked by excessive repression, restrictions on their religious freedom and often violent persecution. They arrived in Hull, then proceeded to Leeds, where my grandfather obtained suitable premises and eventually became one of the principal bakers in the neighbourhood.

My maternal grandparents arrived in London in the early '50s of the last century, not, so far as can be ascertained, because of persecution. They all spoke perfect English and must have had excellent schooling. Their Dutch neighbours had been very tolerant, but the diamond trade in Holland was suffering a recession, so they decided to emigrate to London where the prospects for the diamond cutting and polishing trade were more favourable. The only exception was may maternal grandfather who, in Amsterdam, had been self-employed as a carpenter and glazier and continued his trade in England.

In an orthodox Jewish family it is customary, on the eve of Sabbath, to light candles, say prayers and drink wine. My grandparents were unable to afford luxuries, though sometimes my diamond-cutting uncle, who was better able to afford it, would provide the eve of Sabbath dinner. On many Friday afternoons when I returned from school my grandfather was busy concocting a home-made, although for the purpose quite satisfactory, alternative. He cut up a quantity of raisins, pressed them into a bottle, shook it for a few minutes, and there his wine was. A few of the raisins would sometimes come my way. In addition to the lighted candles on the table there was a large loaf of bread under a white cloth. My grandfather at the head of the table would say a prayer, which to me, with my mind on the bread, seemed unduly long; then he removed the cloth, broke the bread, and gave a piece to each of the people round the table. I later learnt that the ceremony was a thanksgiving to the Almighty for our daily bread. Perhaps also it commemorated the provision of 'manna' when Moses organised the departure of his people from Egypt, and they faced famine in the wilderness.

My maternal grandfather was a lovable character, and although the Dutch were of quick temper and easily roused, I cannot recall a strong word from his lips. He never smoked but chewed vile-looking plugs of tobacco which caused his teeth to look like the Ace of Spades. When I lived in Glasgow and occasionally visited London I would take him some ounces of thick black tobacco, and during my connections with the seafaring fraternity I was able to get this tobacco free of charge as a gift for him. On his Diamond Wedding the family contrived to purchase and present him with a gold watch. He wore it for a couple of days, went for a stroll along Petticoat Lane and returned minus the watch. In those days Petticoat Lane was a hive of pick-pockets; now I dare say it is perhaps more respectable. But was he disturbed by the anger of the family, who showered complaints upon his shoulders because of his loss? Not at all. He had never owned a watch before and regarded it as an encumbrance.

My grandmother made up for my grandfather's mild temper. She was a tall, matriarchal type, exercising stern control over married sons and daughters. No matter what the circumstances they never dared cross swords with her. As I have mentioned, Grandfather had been a carpenter and glazier in Amsterdam, but he found work scarce in London. He would start out in the morning with a frame on his back and small sheets of glass, looking for broken windows of which there were many in the neighbourhood owing to domestic disputes, but there was no fortune to be made, and often he would return home without a penny earned, and be sternly rebuked by my grandmother.

Times were hard and distressing for a great many people. I remember scores of beggars searching the dustbins. Though I could not understand their condition, I thought they looked like clowns in the grotesque garments they wore, presumably for warmth and comfort when sleeping out, and I was rightly rebuked for finding their misery amusing. Near where we lived was an ancient graveyard which had been converted into an open space, a rendezvous for those homeless people. It was known as 'Itchy Park', and we children were warned never to go near it; even the threat of putting us in Itchy Park was frightening enough. It was opposite the Spitalfields fruit market, and the rubbish disposed of saved many beggars and tramps from actual starvation.

Children and many adults went barefoot. There was much drunkenness, not among the Dutch community but certainly among the natives. Gin palaces, as they were called, did good business. I cannot recall my father drinking spirits or beer until some years later in Glasgow. Only when some of our customers met in my father's shop was any alcohol taken. I had not even tasted whisky till I had been an MP for some years.

Apart from family gatherings I do not remember that we had much association with neighbours. Families kept mainly to themselves. There was one exceptional contact. In the summer when fires were unlit, we still had to have hot water for coffee, our main beverage, and it was one of my duties to go with a jug to a house nearby where a widow had a copper (a boiler) in her backyard and sold hot water for a farthing.

Despite the grim life, the squalor of the neighbourhood, and occasional hunger, I must not convey the impression that all was misery during my early childhood. It was exciting to sit and watch one uncle working with what appeared to be two sticks, cutting diamonds, or to be taken by him with some of my younger cousins to the Tower of London or Greenwich Park, and on one memorable Saturday morning paying a visit to Westminster — first to the Abbey, then crossing over to the House of Commons just before ten o'clock, waiting to get in. I do not remember what it was like inside. No doubt at the age of six it failed to arouse my interest, nor could I imagine ever entering the place with some semblance of authority.

I often visited Petticoat Lane, where there was much noise and sometimes scuffling, where competing traders used frightful sounding language and where foods and other goods were being auctioned; eggs at 24 for a shilling and even by one particularly enterprising trader at 36 for a shilling. I have not visited Petticoat Lane more than once or twice in the last fifty years, but as a boy the Lane was to me, despite the dirt, the noise, the squalor and the crowds, exciting, even romantic. One could linger round the fruit and food stalls which had for me the most attraction, because if one looked hungry — I suppose many times I did — the stallholder would hand out an apple or an orange. But the most magnificent jollification came on the Feast of Esther, called Purim, when, long ago, the Jews of Palestine were liberated from an oppressive Persian king. Then the Dutch Tenterground, as it was called, was in high glee. Boys and girls threw bags of flour at each other, for what reason I am unable to say. There was dancing in the streets; stallholders would sell portions of hot peas with vinegar, which cost no more than a halfpenny, and one could buy liver and mash for a penny. This, indeed, was the greatest day of all. There was an atmosphere of poverty, but as a child I was hardly aware of it; I only began to understand it later on.

Then there were the occasions when uncles and aunts with hordes of cousins and in-laws gathered at my grandparents' home at the end of the Sabbath day. When work was plentiful, and in particular when my diamond-cutting uncles were in funds, there would be food in plenty. Young as I was I was conscious of variations in family circumstances. One of my uncles, a brother of my mother, lived in the Mile End Road, in more pleasant accommodation than any we had, either when my father was in London or when we lived with grandparents in his absence. My uncle was a cigar importer and dealer, and when we visited him on occasions I was aware that the surroundings were less dismal and the food better than anything we were accustomed to, though I did not comprehend the reason. There was also an occasion when somebody in my father's family was to be married in Leeds. Somehow rail fares were made available — I expect my parents managed to borrow the money from relatives — and off we went in holiday mood, father, mother, myself and a baby sister. My father's parents in Leeds persuaded him to take a job, and we stayed there for a few weeks until he tired of being too near his father — they never seemed to agree — and we soon found ourselves back in London. This grandfather was not so pleasant as the one in London. He was harsh; always seemed angry. I never liked him.

During our stay in Leeds I was walking along the street where my grandfather kept his grocery shop and bakehouse. (Now the street has vanished and the area is reconstructed.) On the opposite side of the street I saw a policeman, another man and a little girl talking, and the girl was pointing at me. They came over and the girl accused me of stealing some soap which she had bought for her mother that morning. My denial had no effect, so they took me to the nearest police station. I can still see myself, standing at the counter which I could hardly reach and being questioned. They searched me but, of course, no soap was found. All they discovered was a piece of string, an old knife and a catapult, so they let me go, it seemed without a stain on my character, but confiscated the catapult, for which I never have forgiven the Leeds Constabulary. It is interesting to relate that not so long ago some reference to this incident appeared in a newspaper and Rear-Admiral Sir Alexander Gordon Lennox, Serjeant-at-Arms in the House of Commons, decided to commemorate the event by presenting me with a catapult, made by himself, suitably inscribed, which I have in my possession.

When the time came for me to leave the Infants' School, I was sent to a school in Oldcastle Street, just on the fringe of the City near Petticoat Lane, where I stayed for nearly two years. I must have had some education there but I have forgotten what it was. My best memory of the place was of another character. I was something of a favourite with my schoolteacher. She was a young lady who was, I remember, very lovely and often kissed me. I also recall another teacher who decided to form a choir and we had music lessons. At one session she came around and listened to each of her pupils. When she heard my voice she smiled, but apparently not at the thought that I was destined to become a great operatic star. I must confess that in later years it has always been, despite my intense love of music, most distressing to realise that I had no musical accomplishments.

My mother also sent me to learn Hebrew, so I found myself along with a few other boys attending a class run by an old man, whom I best remember not for what he taught me but because he always seemed to be having a cold. We attended twice a week and paid him sixpence every Friday. Regrettably, what I learned does not, in the light of later events, seem to have been of much value. What was important was his regular gift of a farthing to each of us. Now a farthing in those days was not to be sneezed at. For a farthing you could buy a big orange or an ice cream or a bag of nuts. After some months even sixpence became a burden to my mother, and my Hebrew learning terminated.

During my father's frequent absences from London I cannot recall attending any synagogue except when my grandfather would go off on the Sabbath morning and sometimes take me to what was known as the United Synagogue, where the two main sects of Judaism worshipped. These were the Ashkenazi, whose origin was European, and the Sephardic, whose ancestors, believed to be partly Arabic, had lived in comparatively large numbers, before the Inquisition, in Spain and Portugal. Even when my father was in London on the Sabbath he would go off by himself. I learned later that he went somewhere in Whitechapel where many Poles lived, and joined a congregation of those who worshipped in orthodox fashion.

My father's return from the Provinces enabled us to vacate the room in my grandparents' house, and we settled in two rooms of our own. My mother, in accordance with my father's wishes, no longer went out to work, but whether owing to bad trade, or his efforts to form a trade union for the workers in the clothing sweat shops, plus his natural independence, he was out of work again. This time he decided to visit Newcastle, where a brother-in-law had a flourishing grocery business, in the hope of finding something to do. It was suggested that instead of working in the clothing trade he might start a business. He agreed, so they provided him with sufficient funds to open a Seamen's Outfitters shop in South Shields. He was lonely and wanted my mother to join him. As he was unable to write, a friendly neighbour helped. My mother was only too willing; probably she suffered the separation more than he did. But what about rail fares? All he could afford was enough money for a half fare for me. So, at about the age of eight, with a label tied round my neck, I was taken by my mother to Liverpool Street Station and put in charge of the guard on a train to York. This was on the old Great Northern Line before the London and North Eastern Line was constructed. York was the terminus. The guard showed me the utmost kindness and pointed out various places of interest along the line; in particular I remember Lincoln Cathedral. I had to leave the train at York and catch another to Sunderland. After asking several people I found myself in a compartment all by myself. There were no corridor trains in those days. At Sunderland I tried to get out but failed, so I banged at the window and somebody released me. I caught the train for High Shields, and there was my father to meet me.

His business premises consisted of a front shop and one room behind, where we ate, cooked and slept. Sometimes I would be left in charge — between the ages of eight and nine! — while he went aboard vessels in search of customers. My recollection is that the main source of income came from the sale of mattresses to sailors who, in those days on tramp vessels, had to provide their own bedding. He bought several yards of canvas, sewed them up, filled them with straw and sold them for as much as he could get, usually a shilling or fractionally over. On good days he managed to dispose of a second-hand oilskin or a ditty bag in which seamen carried their belongings.

I must refer to an experience in South Shields when I learned something about myself which seemed to have a bearing on my attitude later on. I discovered that I would never be a success as a salesman, nor even capable of making a modest living in that occupation. Our financial circumstances were most depressing and it either occurred to my father, or was suggested to him by his grocer neighbour who was most friendly, and from whom he frequently, no doubt, obtained credit, that he should obtain some goods which we could sell on the nearby beaches during the fine weather. So my father obtained credit from someone in Shields market place, bought a number of articles — spades and buckets and a few toys — and decided that I should take some in a basket, cross by the ferry to Tynemouth (the only means of access from the South to the North of the Tyne) and endeavour to sell them. I had not yet reached the age of nine, and this was my first experience as a petty salesman. However, I crossed by the ferry, and found myself on the amazingly spacious beach where I saw small family groups with many children, and decided to approach them. I exposed my basket of goods, but I said nothing about them, asked no one to buy, just hoped for some response. There was none. After several hours I returned home with the same number of articles in the basket as when I left. Perhaps if I had asked people to buy, they might have done so out of sympathy, but I couldn't ask. This was all the more disappointing because of our financial circumstances.

Some years later when we lived in Glasgow and I was in process of leaving one job for another (my jobs included occasional spells in my father's workshop), he suggested that I should take bundles of cloth and go into the country, particularly among the farming community, and sell them. Apparently the idea was that people would buy the cloth and then my father would visit a potential customer and seek to persuade him to have the cloth made up into suitable garments. He had done so himself. I was then between 14 and 15 years of age. Of course I did as requested, but never sold an inch. The fact is that I lacked the courage to ask anybody to buy.

What bearing had those experiences on my political life? It so happens that in order to become a member of the Glasgow Town Council I was expected to canvass. Fortunately, as it happened, I was so popular in the Fairfield Division of Glasgow that all I required to do was to address one meeting and state my views on matters of local policy to get elected with the highest majority any Council member had achieved. Later, when I became a Parliamentary candidate for the constituency of West Lothian, otherwise known as Linlithgow, midway between Glasgow and Edinburgh, although many of my supporters were charged with the duty of canvassing electors I was never included, though doubtless it was expected of me. The fact is, throughout the whole of my election candidatures, from 1918 when I first stood for Parliament in West Lothian until 1970 when I resigned from the House of Commons after thirty-five years as MP in Seaham and Easington, and also several years in West Lothian, my Scottish constituency, I cannot recall ever canvassing the electors. Speeches from the platform, either indoors or outdoors, I would enjoy and for the most part they were successful. But to knock at doors and ask electors to vote for me was one thing I was incapable of doing. Nor at any time have I approached those in authority, a Prime Minister or a Cabinet Minister, and asked to be appointed to a post in the Government. And the honours too that I have received from time to time have come to me unasked. Some would put it down to pride, vanity or a sense of independence, but I prefer to relate it to my early attempts at salesmanship before the age of nine.

For a while in South Shields it never occurred to my father that my education was being neglected until our kindly grocer neighbour suggested that I should go to school. What education I received I am unable to recall for it lasted no longer than about nine months. What I do recall is that in the same school was a girl about my own age, the daughter of a prosperous ship's chandler, whose premises on the opposite side of the street were vast in comparison to the humble shack we occupied. We walked home together and I must admit to falling in love with her. This boy-and-girl association continued for some time until one day she told me her father objected. He disliked the idea of his daughter talking to the son of a shopkeeper, who obviously was on a much lower income level.

Our business failed to prosper, and one day a friend of my father suggested he might find more suitable employment if he went to Glasgow; so we departed hopefully from South Shields, and I parted from my school girl-friend, which I must confess caused me considerable distress.

2

Growing Up in Glasgow

Whatever my father might have thought of Glasgow — after all, he had had previous experience of the place when he was scouring the country in search of employment — it had no attraction for me. My previous proximity to the North Sea when we lived in South Shields, the Tyne river, the docks and ships, and what was to me a vast sandy beach — at that time one of the most popular seaside resorts of the Durham coast — was a paradise compared to the residence found for us in a grim and squalid-looking building on the banks of the Clyde. I can still recall the area with distaste, even with horror. We had two rooms in a tenement which must have been constructed in the eighteenth or seventeenth century. The sanitary arrangements were appalling, a convenience for three families on each storey. One had frequently to wait until this was vacated, occasionally with very awkward consequences. Baths were unknown: indeed, for many years afterwards if one required a bath apart from the primitive tub one had recourse to the public baths, at twopence for a hot bath. There was also the public swimming bath where I learned to swim; nor should my adopted Scottish patriotism conceal that the famous River Clyde at that time exuded a smell which remained in my nostrils for many years.

Drunkenness seemed to be endemic; on a Saturday night it seemed that every adult male was floating about from one side of the street to the other. But conditions, however unpleasant, had to be endured. What was essential was employment, not readily available, but my father was not lacking in resource and succeeded in obtaining enough work from one of the many clothing establishments to make up suits and other garments, not on their premises but in his own workshop. It was the custom of most clothing firms in Glasgow's main streets to employ outside workers in the absence of other facilities, so he managed to achieve his ambition not to work under an employer, but on his own, and employ help if necessary. I must place on record that although much of the distress he caused to the family was provoked by his remarkably independent character, yet he always sought to help the victims of exploitation; those who were working for starvation wages and suffering abominable conditions. To employ an assistant for the first time in those uncertain economic conditions was worrying, but this had to be faced. Thus my father became an employer; not a prosperous one, but with hope and prospects.

Since our accommodation was limited, one of our two rooms became a workshop by day and a bedroom at night. Housing conditions in Glasgow were far below the standard I had known even in London, although Spitalfields was hardly something to boast about. The singular feature to me in Glasgow was the existence of recesses in most rooms, 'holes in the wall' they were called. These could be curtained off to provide privacy.

I cannot blame my father for our living conditions. He had had a hard upbringing, a harsh father, and no education at all. He had run away from home at the age of twelve, and apart from a brief visit to attend a wedding so far as I know he never returned to his father's home. He was very independent, could not tolerate being bossed. He was severe with me, but when he retired after the age of seventy, I gave him more attention than any other member of the family. He was ninety-three when he died.

I must have been a trial to him as a boy. He took exception to my sports interests. Apart from my association with a junior football club where I played for a time and then was appointed trainer at the age of sixteen, I attended a small gymnasium run by a professional boxer whose younger brother was a chum of mine. We were encouraged to punch a ball, put on boxing gloves and spar around, and sometimes boxed rather forcibly; and when, as sometimes happened, I returned home with two black eyes my father described my behaviour as undignified, and so stifled my ambition to become a champion boxer. His opposition to boxing sent me, instead, to the local library to do some reading. When as a result of my reading and subsequent association with a political organisation I became known as a

Socialist he was even more horrified, even going to the length of destroying some of the pamphlets and papers in my possession.

My father never did any reading, at least till we had lived in Glasgow for some years, but I was fortunate in inheriting a love of reading from my mother. Her romantic nature induced her to buy the penny novelettes popular in those days, and if I gained anything from my education it was more the result of the reading she made available than of anything I learnt at school. Anything romantic in my nature is derived from my beloved mother — my delight in operatic music, the pleasure I had in visiting the Scottish lochs, even my habit of creating an impression of being hard-boiled when in fact I am quite the reverse.

Before long our family situation brightened. Work was more plentiful, money was sufficient to enable my father to send for my mother and baby sister and pay for an assistant. This was a young immigrant from Poland who couldn't speak a word of English, but seemed desperate to learn. This aroused my sympathy and, although just above my ninth year at the time, I tried to help him. This was much welcomed by him and probably contributed to my own education.

Conscious of a neglected education I sought to repair omissions by reading all I could fasten my eyes on. There was no guidance on what to study or how to apply the knowledge gained. No doubt help was available; but I was too independent, or vain, to ask for it. Yet there was compensation in my readiness to listen to those whose knowledge was superior to my own. This still persists; even in my advanced age I am an intense listener. If I possess any claim to be an effective debater — as has been acknowledged — it is because I enjoy the oratory and debating skill of others more able than myself. I admit that in no speech delivered by me, even though compliments were numerous, have I gained complete satisfaction. A wrong turn of phrase, a superfluous sentence, a superficial statement of facts, or it could be excessive declamation, would cause me a sleepless night: to aspire to perfection was my aim in speech and numerous activities in which I have had the privilege to play some part. In the search for perfection my public life is one of persistent correction. Otherwise, how could I have overcome the obstacles that confronted me in all the turbulent years?

Out of the blue, one day — I never understood why — my

mother said, 'You're going to school.' Now I had not been to school since leaving South Shields and I was not eager to return. All the same, she took me along to the Adelphi Terrace Public School, about half a mile from where we lived. When we got to the place I clung to the railings and refused to enter, yelling my head off. My mother was the stronger, and, after a struggle, I found myself before a large man who asked me several questions which I failed to understand. He had a pronounced Glasgow brogue, much too harsh for me. Besides, I was too shy to respond. Mother left me with a promise to return and, meanwhile, I was taken to a classroom and given a seat at a small desk. No account was taken of my brief schooling in London and even less in South Shields. It seemed that I was put into a class suited to my age, and I was acutely distressed when, along with other children, I was expected to answer questions on a subject about which I knew nothing. We were asked to write in an exercise book what we considered were suitable answers. What could I do? I did what I suppose was shameful. I tried several times to look over the shoulder of a boy in the desk below me. But it was no use; the teacher must have realised by my movements that something was wrong. A few days later, in a new and lower class, I gradually adapted myself to the situation. We were one day examined not by our own teacher but by a man whom the teacher introduced as the Visiting Inspector. He examined us in mental arithmetic and other subjects and I speedily responded. He was impressed and remarked, 'That boy has his head screwed on straight.' This is the sole commendation I ever received in my limited education.

One other vivid and disturbing experience was my gradual awareness of poverty in the Gorbals part of Glasgow. We had our share of it until work became more plentiful, though I am unable to recall any prolonged period when we were short of food. Gorbals, on the South side of the Clyde, was inhabited by many Jewish immigrant families and also by those who had left various Continental countries for Britain as far back as the early part of the nineteenth century. The older families, engaged mainly in the clothing and furniture business, were doing very well. Some travelled around the towns and villages in the West of Scotland and even up to the Highlands peddling their wares. Some Jewish families whose names are now household words and are reputed to be extremely wealthy, laid the foundations of their fortunes in Glasgow and the West of Scotland. But for the most part the Jewish community had to rely on the charity of those who could afford it. Charity and benevolence are traditional among Jewish people.

Often my father would ask me to look after his small shop in Glasgow's East End when he found it more profitable to travel in the countryside and sell cloth and sometimes persuade purchasers to have the cloth made up. As for selling much in the shop I was hopeless. I would often also have to travel to places several miles from Glasgow to deliver clothes made in the workshop. One reason for sending me instead of using parcel post or rail was to receive immediate payment. On one occasion I had to deliver two suits to a mining village near Falkirk. It was about two miles outside the town and the name was strange to me; it was called California, hardly a village, just a hamlet with a few houses, an uphill walk from Falkirk — and my parcel was fairly heavy. However, I found the tiny cottage where the customer, a middle-aged woman, lived. The suits were for her two sons, and when I entered, she was preparing food for them to take to the pit. This consisted of two thick chunks of bread sandwiched with thick slices of cheese and covered with marmalade. This attracted me so much that I tried it later for myself, and it has remained a habit with me ever since, particularly when I prefer not to have a full meal. I should not be surprised if my sturdy constitution, and on the whole fairly good health, owe something to that day in the remote hamlet of California. What was even more important at the time was payment for the clothes on the spot.

I also made several visits to Motherwell, where my father had a friend who had a flourishing business. He was interested in me when I came to deliver parcels, and told me he was a vegetarian. For years he had never tasted meat, and said this was the reason for his good health. For purposes of economy, which became necessary after my marriage when I was unemployed, I tried vegetarianism and practised it for quite a long period. It is perhaps regrettable that when my financial circumstances improved I abandoned it and went back to a normal diet.

More directly important for my character formation even

than formal education, was — and still is — my habit of observing what other people do: curiosity about their style of living, listening to what they say, assessing their character and quality, their likes and dislikes, and, above all, in their periods of success or failure, even rumours and allegations of improper behaviour, seeking always for the motivation in their activities, even to the extent of probing into their thoughts. Let me quote a passage from two of my favourite poems, which could summarise my conception of a civilised existence. One, on the need for caution and scepticism, is from Omar Khayyam:

> Myself, when young did eagerly frequent,
> Doctor and Saint and heard great argument
> About it and about: but evermore
> Came out by the same door wherein I went.

The other, on the quality of compassion, which a few lines of verse can equal, is by Robert Burns:

> Then gently scan your brother man,
> Still gentler sister woman;
> Though they may gang a'kenning wrang,
> To step aside is human.

Forgive the digression and let us proceed with the narrative.

Many Gorbals residents were Roman Catholics, immigrants from Southern Ireland, labourers in the nearby steelworks, at the docks, in building and, among the better off, publicans, pawnbrokers and shopkeepers. On the whole, relations between Jews and the Irish were friendly, except when the latter got too much drink and then, if an Irishman considered he had got a raw deal from a Jew with whom he had business, he became troublesome. Of course there was some anti-semitism owing to jealousy, when some Jews were flourishing and showing off a bit, but far more because some of the more ignorant and bigoted of the Catholics could never forgive the Jews for having crucified Christ. How often did I hear the story about the Irishman who saw an elderly Jew in the street and gave him a punch on the jaw. When the Jew protested and asked the reason for the assault, the reply was 'You crucified Christ'. 'But,' said the old Jew, 'that was nearly 2,000 years ago.' 'Ah!' said the Irishman, 'I only heard it yesterday.'

The women of the working class, almost without exception, wore shawls, but seldom hats, and the men always wore caps. They were badly dressed, bought second-hand clothes in a place called Paddy's Market, where plenty of discarded rubbish was on sale. The poverty-stricken workers, far too often unemployed and, even when in work, receiving wages below subsistence level, seldom got a new suit or a new dress unless on credit, although a man's suit could be bought then for ten shillings and a dress for five. They simply could not afford more.

Like many other working-class children I usually went about with bare feet, except at school where I wore a cheap kind of shoe made partly of canvas and rubber which cost about one shilling or at most one and sixpence. When things were looking up I got a new suit, sometimes made in the workshop, but when father was too busy he might buy me one for a small sum, although even this was not always possible.

Recollection of the squalor still lingers in my memory. Glasgow Corporation, now associated with Strathclyde, is one of the most enlightened local authorities, but in the early '90s of last century the sanitary arrangements, the scarcity of adequate toilets and also the accumulation of filth in the streets were not entirely the fault of the Council. The vermin, rats, cockroaches, bed bugs, etc., together with lack of proper nutrition among the workers, were largely responsible for the disease, the occasional epidemics and the rickety legs which were familiar in the streets of Glasgow. Infant mortality was at a high level, probably higher than in most industrial towns. Tuberculosis was common and thousands suffered from it.

The dreadful housing conditions were mostly to blame and this was frequently the theme of speeches by progressive members and candidates for membership of the City Council. Private landlords were unable or unwilling to help. Some complained that the tenants were to blame because of their inability to cope with conditions, and their excessive drinking and manner of living. The more enlightened argued that unless the slums were demolished disease would increase. It was this which led to the provision of Council estates, in spite of being for many years hotly opposed by private landlords; some had their representatives on the Council.

19

The time came when my father decided that more accommodation was essential in order to handle the growing volume of work, so off we went to live in the rather more respectable Gallowgate, near Glasgow Cross, the centre of the city. By this time father had obtained work from some of the larger clothing stores and was able to employ a cutter and a few other workers. The accommodation both for living and work was more ample; we were now better off; but what about my schooling? I was just over eleven, and had not returned to Adelphi Terrace School for several weeks, largely owing to our change of residence. The school was some distance away, but my sister and I went back for a time and my mother arranged with a dairy near the school to provide us with bread and a glass of milk during the mid-day break. But when the weather turned colder it was decided that neither of us should return. By this time I was about eleven years and six months old. Attendance Officers were not as active as they appear to be at present. No enquiry was made. It suited my sister and myself not to return to school; so I became an errand boy while she helped in the kitchen.

I was sent with parcels to the shops with clothes made up in the workshop and sometimes to private customers. One day I had to deliver a parcel in Springburn in the Northern part of Glasgow. I could travel by bus or tram, but there was a railway station opposite where we lived so I decided to go to Springburn by train. I was given sixpence for my fare. At the station I found the cost was sixpence for first class and fourpence for third, so, to the astonishment of the clerk — I can still see his shocked face — I asked for a first-class ticket for sixpence. Why I did it I don't know. It may have been curiosity, or an intuition that I was to join the rather better-off members of the community.

3

Education out of School

My father had his plans about my future; I must train to be a tailor's cutter, regarded as the aristocrat of the tailoring trade. After a few lessons I was convinced it was not for me. Anyway, I could not concentrate and my teacher, a cutter employed by my father, was of the same opinion. I was twelve years of age; but I was not long out of work. I applied for and got a job with F. & J. Smith, a well-known tobacco firm. It was to deliver parcels of tobacco and the pay was four shillings a week. In rain or shine I had to be out and often got very wet, but promotion was not far away and the foreman responsible for dispatch asked if I would like to go on their van instead of walking. I agreed and was promoted to van boy at five shillings a week. My job was to sit at the back of the van and jump off when we came to the place of delivery. The hours were from eight-thirty to six o'clock, and we were allowed a mid-day break of half an hour. I couldn't go home for lunch (we called it dinner in those days; the term lunch was never used in our circles), but next door to the factory there was a baker's shop where they sold broken cake and biscuits for a penny a bag. During all the time I worked there I cannot remember having anything else for the mid-day break. The size of the bag depended on the girl who served you. Some girls would give you more than others, so I always looked for the girl who I knew was good for a big bag. Often if we reached the factory late, having finished about seven, I helped to put away the van and the horse.

My wanderings around Glasgow, delivering parcels of tobacco, and in particular when travelling on the van, increased my understanding of the kind of city Glasgow then was. Occasionally we took parcels to firms in the city centre, where the business and professional gentlemen bought their requirements. Trade in those shops was brisk; their customers were usually pipe smokers. Some smoked clay pipes — I remember our doctor who would fish into the back pocket of his frock coat, which most doctors of the time wore, and produce his clay pipe — but many smoked cigarettes and also cigars. They were well dressed, wore bowler hats and carried umbrellas. Only a few, and strange-looking, motor cars were seen in those days, but there were many fine carriages, and in some of the principal streets, like Sauchiehall and Buchanan Streets, fine shops displaying expensive goods; there was no sign of the poverty of Gorbals and the docks area or the East End. Even in the extensive district of Gorbals away from the Clyde there were fewer slums and people were better dressed. Schoolchildren exemplified the difference. It was only in the worst parts that one could see bare-footed children. Also there were fewer men hanging about street corners, unlike the unemployed seen in Crown Street and Main Street in the Gorbals, and around Glasgow Green across the river and the Salt Market. There were two Glasgows, one looked rich and comfortable, the other extremely impoverished. I belonged to the latter.

When we moved to the Gallowgate, although the tenements looked as grim as those we had left in Adelphi Terrace and on the banks of the Clyde, the shops were busier and Glasgow didn't seem such a depressing place after all. But we were not intended for a prolonged stay in the Gallowgate. Again my father was on his wanderings, this time to take a vacant shop in the East End of Glasgow in a quarter largely populated by Irish people. The shop was near a Roman Catholic chapel and practically all our neighbours belonged to that persuasion. We occupied two rooms and a kitchen on the second floor of an adjacent tenement. My father stocked the shop with ready-made suits, odd trousers and vests. It was quite common to see men wearing suits consisting of a different cloth for the jacket, trousers and waistcoat.

At the rear of the shop was a workshop which became rendezvous for customers who had become friendly with my father. Most were from the South of Ireland, but a few came from Ulster, who were Protestants and associated with the Orange Order. They would occupy the workshop at night and consume plenty of whisky, which they brought or my father provided. When it was disposed of they would send me to a public house for more. Thus I began my political education. The usual discussions were about the years of English oppression of the Irish. My father, who was completely ignorant of Irish history, never intervened; he found it diplomatic to be reticent and agree with his customers; but when they made rude remarks about the monarchy and were cynical about any favourable reference to the Union Jack, I would intervene. This was regarded with disfavour by my father, who was more concerned with retaining custom than encouraging my patriotic sentiments. During the Boer War when the Civic Volunteers, partly voluntary though impelled by unemployment, were formed, the discussions in the workshop became pro-Boer, but those were not my sentiments, particularly when I saw the men marching to the docks en route to South Africa, and my patriotism was aroused forcefully. Then I got strict instructions either to be quiet or clear out.

Sometimes a schoolmaster from the nearby Roman Catholic school paid us a visit. He was also a customer and though he engaged in the discussions was rather more moderate than the others when it looked as if debate would end in a 'donnybrook'. He was interested in me and advised me to visit the library and read various books, which I promised to do, though my interest in sport seemed more important. Perhaps the most exciting time was when another customer introduced a note of patriotism. He was an Orangeman. Then nothing but liberal doses of whisky would lower the temperature. It was during these discussions that I learned how witty the Irish can be. One old fellow, whose origins were in Southern Ireland, would remark: 'I'm never well when I eat too much, but I am worse the day I eat too little.' And another said, 'I don't mind what they tax me so long as I have the income.'

I found the Orangeman customer still more interesting when he told how, on a Saturday when he hadn't enough money to take his suit out of pawn, he kept up appearances by putting on his only stiff shirt — very common in those days — and leaning out of his window, concealing the fact that he was still wearing his moleskin trousers, which he wore all week when working. The custom of pawning Sunday clothes on Monday and taking them out of pawn on Saturday, provided there was enough left out of wages, was only too common. Occasionally some of the priests from the local chapel would drop in. Most of them had their clothes repaired in the workshop; like lay members of their church they seldom had enough money to buy a new suit or coat. They were most friendly towards us and never attempted to convert my father. Politics, relating to the Irish problems, yes, but religion was never mentioned.

After leaving the job of van boy with the tobacco firm I had several jobs. One was in a chair-making factory. I had to get up about five o'clock in the morning and be at work at six. My job was to heat the glue pot, put some glue in the holes in the base of the chairs, and put sticks into them. But this did not last long; my mother disliked my going to work so early in the morning. Then they tried to apprentice me to a pastry maker, but at the last minute my father thought I should stay in the workshop.

This led to a row with him so, one morning, instead of going to the workshop, I left and walked to Dalmuir seven miles away, and applied for a job at the Singer Sewing Machine factory. Some of my chums already worked there and boasted about the high wages they got. Singer's was then known to pay the highest wages around Glasgow. I saw a foreman, asked for a job, and was told to start on Monday at seventeen shillings a week. Although not yet fifteen, I looked big for my age, but that did not seem to matter. I got back to Glasgow towards evening, having had only some bread and tea all day, and hung about until some chums arrived at the street corner where we used to gather. I told them what I had done, and then arose the question of where I would stay the night. After some discussion they decided they would collect enough to enable me to go to one of the model lodging houses in the neighbourhood. The collection amounted to ninepence, just enough to pay for lodgings for one night. But before the deal was concluded my mother, who had been searching all over for me, came along and I was taken home by the scruff of the neck. I was certain the old man would give me a hiding, but he was so relieved that I had turned up that all I got was something to eat.

On another occasion when we had a row I ran away and went to the Recruiting Office in the Gallowgate and asked to join the Navy. I was measured, found to be the right height, and all seemed well until they informed me that my parents' consent was necessary because I was under fifteen. That settled my chance of joining the Navy, but this time I got more than I bargained for on my arrival home. You can never tell; I might have become an Admiral many years later instead of Minister of Defence!

Although, as I have said, I was advised to go to the library, I remained more interested in sport, still taking part in boxing and playing football with club members aged fourteen to sixteen in a field near the ground used by Glasgow Celtic in the Parkhead district.

My activities were not however confined to football, athletics, and visits to a gymnasium where I could punch a ball and try my hand at heavyweight lifting. Usually, on a Saturday night, I would visit the City Hall where concerts were held at a cost equivalent to threepence in our present currency. The price included a bag of sweets. There I enjoyed performances by vocalists who, in later years, became famous. Great artistes like Harry Lauder and Will Fyffe made their reputations at those concerts, and were content to receive no more than a guinea in payment! And one could obtain a gallery seat in the Theatre Royal for a few pence and be thrilled to listen to popular operas such as *Pagliacci, Cavalleria Rusticana* and *La Bohème*.

Then began, with my scanty financial resources, the purchase of books, usually second-hand, Dickens, Thackeray, Walter Scott, Thomas Hardy, and also some of the writings of French and Russian authors, Zola, Hugo, Maupassant, Tolstoy, Gogol and Gorky. Owing to my father's opposition to boxing, I did eventually visit the Central Library in Miller Street, and selected books from the catalogue whose contents I usually failed to understand.

There was an occasion when my chum suggested we should go to the Queen's Music Hall round the corner from Glasgow Cross, where an American was appearing who claimed to be the world's greatest illusionist. My chum was interested in conjuring tricks and hoped to learn something. We paid fourpence each for seats in the pit and sat through some third-rate dancing and singing. Then the illusionist appeared on the stage and after pretending to saw a women in half and performing some amazing card tricks announced that the most amazing feat of all was about to begin. He asked for six chairs to be placed on the stage, invited six members of the audience to occupy the chairs and assured us that he would, by touching the chairs with his fingers, produce electricity. My chum was one of those who accepted the invitation. The illusionist stood behind each of the chairs, touched them with his fingers and each of the six persons jumped up as if he had got a shock. Naturally, the audience applauded; electricity was something new and the magician was using no instrument. My chum returned beside me, looking as pale as a ghost, so I asked, 'What happened to you? Did you get a shock?' He just shook his head. He could hardly speak. I said, 'Did he stick a pin in you?' 'No,' he muttered. I said, 'What happened to you? You jumped.' He replied, 'He just leaned over me and said, "Jump, you bugger, jump," and what could I do?' Is it any wonder that I was disillusioned so early in life; became sceptical and cautious about what I read or heard?

Another revealing incident occurred when I was sent to deliver a parcel to a shop just outside the Glasgow area. There I found the air was much fresher; in the distance were many trees, and it all seemed so different from where I lived. So, instead of returning, I walked on and came to a narrow lane and saw for the first time hedges covered with roses. I learned later they were wild roses. I was thrilled and stood gazing at them, and would have picked some but they were full of thorns. In all the years that have passed since — just about eighty — I have never forgotten the sight of that hedge; I had no idea that such lovely things existed. I have to admit that despite the pleasure gained, and the brief escape from the familiar environment, I cheated on my return from my errand. Rebuked for being so long, I excused myself by saying I had lost my way. I had never witnessed anything so beautiful in the London parks where my uncle took us for a Saturday morning stroll, or in Shields. It was the urge to see more of this that inspired my frequent walks later. On many occasions I would walk from Glasgow to Balloch, on the shores of Loch Lomond, or to the Campsie Hills, both a longish trek by any standards. When asked about my hobbies, I have said walking and talking. The benefit I derived from my job for the Labour Pary from 1931 to 1935 was certainly not the money: it was the long walks.

My employment was never regular or secure, but the same

would apply to thousands of other young people and many adults. It was only between the outbreak of war in 1914 and its termination in 1918 that industry was operating on the highest level and work was regular, but during the period following the Boer War, around 1903, until my marriage, employment was irregular. Very few of the workshops engaged in the ready-made, off-the-peg trade — the smaller master tailors — worked on Monday or even on Tuesday; often they depended on the flow of orders, which led to a feverish rush near the end of the week.

I reckon I worked on and off for at least a dozen employers from the age of twelve. I was never fully employed until engaged at the age of twenty-five by the Scottish Co-operative Wholesale Society about the year 1907 in their Shieldhall factory. Even there we had occasional periods of idleness; odd days laid off when stocks were piling up and orders were few. On the other hand, if one cared to accept temporary employment in a small workshop it was possible, in the rush of business and in working long hours, with only two or three days in the week, to earn wages far in excess of those I earned in more regular employment. Often one was asked to take a job with a master tailor who employed no more than two or three workpeople, or sometimes asked to help out and work late through the day and part of the night to complete orders for which one could earn ten shillings a day — in present currency worth fifty pence! Even with a full week's work in the Shieldhall factory the weekly wage was never more than thirty-five shillings. There were occasions from 1908 to 1911 when I would be asked to do two or three days' work for a master tailor, admittedly working long hours, and earn as much as three pounds, much more than the average skilled artisan in engineering and shipbuilding, whose wages, apart from overtime, seldom were more than two pounds.

4

Dawn of a Political Conscience

Poor business in the shop and my father's usual unrest induced him to accept a job as manager of a small clothing factory in South Shields. The Glasgow shop was closed and the rest of the family departed for the new home. I decided to remain in Glasgow. I took lodgings with a lady who provided me with a room and breakfast for a few shillings a week. The breakfast usually consisted of bread, tea and sardines. Sometimes there would be an egg. But after she had boiled the egg she used the water to make the tea.

Then Father wrote and asked me to come and work for him. There seemed few prospects in Glasgow, so off I went to Shields. I did not have enough for the rail fare, so he sent me some money, but I decided to travel by sea which was much cheaper than the train. I went to Leith to get a boat to Newcastle. I shall never forget how seasick I was; the North Sea must have been at its worst. There was no cabin accommodation except for the first-class passengers, so I lay on deck throughout the night. It was a relief to arrive at Newcastle Quay.

Though no great shakes as a boxer I knew something about the game and soon displayed my prowess on my return to South Shields. This brought a suggestion to one of my chums and myself to join a boxing booth. I might have agreed, but before leaving Glasgow I had become friendly with a young lady with whom I now corresponded. When no longer employed by my father (he never liked my work, and I hated it) she suggested my return to Glasgow where I could find work without much difficulty. Moreover, I was convinced that the kind of environment encountered in South Shields could have had, in time, a corrupting influence on me. The problem was how to get to

Glasgow; I had to find the money.

When I left Glasgow I took with me a trunk of books and picked up many from second-hand stalls in Shields market place. These included works by Dickens, Thackeray, Walter Scott and other novelists of the period, also several dealing with travel, in which I was intensely interested. I also had some semi-scientific books, such as Haeckel's *Riddle of the Universe* and Herbert Spencer's *Sociology*. I also recall Paley's *Evidences of Christianity*; but have no idea why I purchased it except perhaps through my innate curiosity. So off I went to the market place and arranged for a bookseller to buy the lot. He was only prepared to pay twopence each. However, that was enough to pay my fare to Glasgow, and for the second time I departed from Shields. I hoped I had finished with the place, but some years later when I was National Organiser of the Marine Workers' Union, Shields was one of the ports included in my itinerary.

I returned to my former lodgings in Glasgow at a slightly higher price but unfortunately with the same kind of breakfast. I confess that the widow, my landlady, although somewhat older than myself, may have had notions about me. She certainly did her best for me but I could never become reconciled to her using the egg water for my tea.

Until then I had not the least interest in politics. I was convinced, in my innocence, that all the troubles that beset the world, including the squalor, the slums and the impoverishment in Glasgow, could be resolved by scientific research. Then I made a trade union connection. I was advised to associate myself with a union formed by Jewish clothing workers. Before deciding I attended one of their meetings and concluded that an ethnic trade union was inadvisable. Whatever their origin their association should be with the general body of trade unionists. The following statement expressed my views:

> Organisations of Jewish workers have sprung into existence in as little time as it takes to tell, and have as quickly died away.
>
> Now, right here, let me say that independent organisations composed exclusively of Jewish workers, whether as a means of improving conditions of trade, raising rates, or even maintaining the 'status quo' are absolutely futile. Their methods of fighting, their

ignorance of trade union law, the social relationship between master and man, and the independent position of the small Jewish employer, all serve to render the efforts of Jewish trade unionists to improve their position of no avail.

Now, the question arises, what is to be the future of Jewish organisation in this country? Is the outlook favourable or gloomy? Does there appear to be any possibility of effective organisation among them? My personal opinion is that the immediate future of Jewish organisation is extremely unfavourable. The Jewish worker is passing through a process of trade union education and experience which will eventually teach him that his emancipation will come not through organisations based on racial sentiment, but from combinations of working men, whether they be Gentile or Jew, based on fellowship and human understanding in which the barriers of racial and religious intolerance have been transcended. But that time is not yet.

The time will come when through the exigencies of the industrial system and bitter experience they will gladly seek our help. When it does, I trust that the hand of fellowship will be extended so that Jew and Gentile may be able to work together for the emancipation of the human race.

Where I worked there was a branch of one of the garment workers' unions. I joined and before long became keenly interested, taking part in discussions at branch meetings, and listened to lectures by important officials who paid us visits. We also had some exiles from Russia and Poland, who spoke in their own language, which was translated. This was during a period of many pogroms in Russia and in Poland, alongside rumours of possible revolution in those countries. After listening to these people, and our own officials, I gained some knowledge of industrial affairs and the cause of vast emigration. I also visited the Speakers' Forum at Glasgow Green where nightly, and always at weekends, large crowds gathered and engaged in animated discussions on various topics, in particular religion and local politics. Often disputes between Roman Catholics and Orangemen ended in fisticuffs. I remember a speaker for the Orange cause who said bitter things about Rome and, pointing to his black eye, remarked: 'This is their only effective argument.' Speakers who talked on political subjects I ignored.

Those who preached Socialism still failed to interest me; I had not the faintest idea what it meant. One day, however, I was engaged in a dispute with someone much older than myself about the origin of the universe, no doubt displaying my ignorance of the subject, when suddenly somebody pushed his way in and told me I was talking nonsense. It was in his opinion Socialism that mattered; but I was convinced that science would eventually solve all our problems. Even then, however, I was conscious that my knowledge on this or any other subject was superficial.

The term 'science' in my education is a misnomer. In the course of my frequent visits to the Speakers' Forum, then one of our largest open spaces, I listened to speakers who, for the most part, advocated their views on theology. At the outset what occasioned surprise was that they all claimed to be fully seized of the virtues of Christianity but attacked each other with the utmost vigour, sometimes with physical violence. I always avoided debate on religion. Though not at first a Socialist, I was concerned about local politics, housing, social conditions, etc. This, I confess, confused me until some person, shabbily dressed but with a cultured accent, engaged in argument with the religious element, spoke of the universe in terms which appeared to be the antithesis of what the advocates of religion had expressed. I found his arguments difficult to understand, but they became more interesting when he suggested I might attend meetings of the Glasgow Secular Society, which met every Sunday morning, and listen to their various orators. Even so, I gained limited understanding of their arguments. Then, having read Haeckel's *Riddle of the Universe* I sought to understand what was described as the monistic philosophy, the existence of innumerable planets, the illimitable universe; the subject of creation and man's place in the universe. This was followed up by occasional visits to the Kelvingrove Art Gallery where there existed a vast number of glass cases containing relics of the past; skeletons of mammals and fossils, which could be interpreted in historical terms.

I must confess that my confusion, listening to the advocates of religion in the Forum and gaining no further knowledge about Judaism, occurred because, apart from the few early years when I lived in Glasgow, we always resided in areas where hardly a single member of the Jewish persuasion lived. No doubt that environment had some effect. Before I was sixteen there were occasional visits to a synagogue in the West End of Glasgow, where my father would take me, not on Sabbath day, but only on the occasion of the Jewish New Year and what he regarded as more important, Yom Kippur, the Day of Atonement. But before I was seventeen the family had left Glasgow for South Shields, so I lived by myself, without any association with members of the Jewish community apart from my acquaintance with the young lady who subsequently became my wife. When I was introduced to her family they seemed anything but favourable to her association with someone who, by then, was alleged to have become a Socialist. Yet at the time I had not the slightest conception of what Socialism meant. However, my knowledge of science, whether theoretical or applied, was of the most limited character, except that it seemed to me that scientific research into the subject of creation was more likely to help in the solution of the problems at the time than the slogans that were associated with political parties. I was curious and wanted to know what was the world about and what was life for.

Even when I joined a trade union — and that was only when I had returned to Glasgow from South Shields and had joined a trade union on the advice of a friend — I failed to associate the trade union with politics. It was more a protest against unemployment, and the miserable wages paid to those in work. Of course I had listened to political discussion in my father's workshop during the Boer War, between those who were loyal to the Crown and those who were the descendants of the Southern Irish, who despised England and expressed themselves in the most disloyal terms. At the time I was patriotic, more particularly when I saw men marching to the docks on their way to South Africa, though I could hardly be expected to understand the reason for their departure, and I suspect my patriotism was of the subconscious variety — I just believed Britain was the best country.

Having obtained some useful employment, I spent much of my spare time in the public library. Looking through the catalogue, I came across the *Meditations* of Marcus Aurelius, and I venture a favourite passage:

> In the morning when thou findest thyself unwilling to rise, consider with thyself presently, it is to go about a man's work that I am stirred up. Am I then yet unwilling to go about that, for which I myself was born and brought forth into this world? Or was I made for this, to lay me down, and make much of myself in a warm bed?
>
> Think thyself fit and worthy to speak, or to do anything that is according to nature, and let not the reproach, or report of some that may ensue upon it, ever deter thee. If it be right and honest to be spoken or done, undervalue not thyself so much, as to be discouraged from it.

There was so much to read, study and meditate about, which I had missed in my so-called schooldays. Naturally I was interested in scientific topics, but could not ignore famous authors like George Borrow, whose writings were like a breath of fresh air. I quote:

> There's night and day, brother, both sweet things; sun, moon and stars, brother, all sweet things; there's likewise a wind on the heath. Life is very sweet, brother; who would wish to die?
>
> There's a wind on the heath, brother; if I could only feel that, I would gladly live for ever.

And naturally, searching for the speeches by the founder of the Independent Labour Party, Keir Hardie, I discovered an unexpected eloquence. Hardie suffered from repeated illness. During one of his rest cures he wrote the following:

> Outside the twinkling stars are keeping watch over the silent world. What a blessed thing is the holy calm of this home retreat. Not a sound to be heard save the slow tick of the old grandfather clock on the stairs and the soothing murmur of the Lugar water at the foot of the garden. London is a place I remember almost with horror, as if I had been confined there once in the long ago. The weary feet on the pavement, the raucous song, the jingle of cabhorse bells.

The man who had intervened in Glasgow Green, I subsequently discovered, was Neil McLean, who was at that time a member of the Socialist Labour Party, which was the forerunner of the Communist Party. He became an MP for Labour in 1918. McLean produced a pamphlet, *Wage, Labour and Capital* by Karl Marx, and told me to read it. I took it away, but failed for some time to get its meaning. However, what I did understand was that everywhere workers were exploited by Capitalists and that, to me, appeared to be an injustice. Then I made the acquaintance of the writings of Robert Blatchford, not only the *Clarion*, of which he was Editor, but one of his books, *Britain for the British*, which I believe sold a million copies. Robert Blatchford was a remarkable character who exercised more influence on my political outlook than any other. His writings persuaded the Glasgow Trades' Council, the most influential Labour organisation in the West of Scotland, to invite him to come and speak and I was asked to take the Chair.

Before I joined the Independent Labour Party in 1903 I had heard of the *Clarion*. Although I did not subscribe to it weekly, occasionally I had the opportunity of reading it in the public library. This led me to purchase some of the books written by Blatchford — *Britain for the British*, *Merry England* and *Not Guilty*. The price of these books was one shilling but both *Britain for the British* and *Merry England* Blatchford decided to sell at a cost of one penny. They actually sold in thousands and probably had more influence in directing people's thoughts to radical ideas than anything produced by other organisations connected with the Socialist Movement, like the Fabian Society and the Social Democratic Federation. Blatchford was no orator, but his language was simple, clear-cut, easily understood and for a person like myself, with limited education, more likely to be of value in forming ideas than the writings and speeches of some of the Labour politicians of the period, Keir Hardie among them.

I first met Keir Hardie, regarded rightly as one of the principal founders of the Labour Movement, when some of my colleagues of the ILP met in one of Glasgow's tea rooms. Of course I had heard and read much about him, admired his resolution, courage and integrity, though I was not so readily influenced by his speeches or writings as I was by those of Robert Blatchford who aroused the sentiments of the working class and social reformers to a height far in excess of anything contributed by Hardie, however well-meaning and sincere the latter was. Hardie was a man of undoubted sincerity but was inclined to be dictatorial, and frequently gave offence to other prominent members of the Labour Movement like Ramsay

MacDonald, Arthur Henderson, of the political wing, and Tom Mann and Ben Tillett, two of the most prominent trade union leaders. Disputes among political leaders are commonplace. The Labour Party has had more than a fair share of them: it still continues. In any assessment of Keir Hardie's quality and contribution, one cannot ignore the dismal conditions of his upbringing; his struggles on behalf of the Ayrshire miners and, regrettably, his recurring bouts of illness. If, for me, Robert Blatchford was the most profound influence it was largely owing to the clear-cut, concise and easily understood language used by Blatchford in comparison with the somewhat prosy, economic jargon which was far too often Hardie's contribution. Although Blatchford was not recognised by the official Labour Movement as an authority on Socialist philosophy and economics, his writings were more favourably received by the working classes. His contribution to Socialist progress was exceptional. There was the additional factor of Blatchford's humour and his having been a sergeant in the British Army which was more consistent with my romantic sentiments.

So rapidly did my Socialist education improve that six months later I was engaged in a debate in the Glasgow Forum on Socialism with a man much older than myself who was an experienced debater. This took place in the adjoining Bird Market, before a crowd of over five hundred. There were no seats; all were standing. At the end I received much applause, and the promoters of the meeting gave me ten shillings out of the collection. This was the only fee I ever got for taking part in Socialist propaganda. So, between the age of eighteen and nineteen I emerged as something of a Socialist, with a limited knowledge of the subject, yet with confidence as a debater. But I had interests other than debating; I had become engaged to the young lady I corresponded with when in South Shields and who became my wife. She had accepted me but I regret to say her family had not. They objected to anybody in the family marrying a Socialist.

It is difficult for those engaged in political life, even prominent members of the Labour Party, to understand how we were regarded by the public in those days. Socialists, they declared, were all atheists; they wanted to upset society and rob the people of their savings. We were also suspected of believing in free love. In fact we were the sort of people who ought to be shot at sight. Such impressions were common despite the association with Labour and Socialism of many clergymen and prominent personalities like Bernard Shaw, Sydney Webb and other famous people.

The end of the Boer War plunged Britain into a severe trade recession, and thousands of workers found themselves out of a job. Nobody believed that our military adventures in South Africa had improved our prestige. The war had not been popular with the Labour Party nor even with the Liberal Party, then the only possible rival to the Tories. The Labour Party in embryo had just been formed at a conference of trade unions, the Independent Labour Party, the Social Democratic Federation and a number of Liberals who met in London in 1900. The intention was, certainly on the part of Keir Hardie, Ben Tillett, Tom Mann and prominent Socialists, to form a working-class Labour Party, but eventually they restricted their demand to Labour representation in Parliament in order to legalise the operation of trade unions. Actually, the Parliamentary Labour Party was not formed until 1906 when they created an Executive Council.

The Movement was making much ground in Glasgow and the West of Scotland and produced a crop of propagandists whose names became almost household words. There was the acknowledged leader, Keir Hardie himself, there was Bruce Glazier, Ramsay MacDonald, Philip Snowden and perhaps the most famous of all I have mentioned, Robert Blatchford, whose writings were now beginning to influence many people not only among the workers but in the professions, although many of the unemployed and poverty-stricken workers refused to have anything to do with Labour or Socialism. The periodical *Clarion* formed an organisation known as the Clarion Scouts, whose members held meetings at street corners and at park gates. I decided to join them and at first became a member of their Speakers' Class. Before long I found myself addressing meetings, usually on a Saturday afternoon, and as far away as Coatbridge, Motherwell and other towns in Lanarkshire. I must admit, though, that I was a bit of a novice at the game. My knowledge of Socialist philosophy was still superficial, but I made up for it by fulminations against society for allowing thousands of people to suffer the ills of poverty, to live in the slums and without any security. It was the need for social justice I was preaching. This made some impact on the minds of my audience. My indignation was reinforced by the unemployment which I suffered myself.

The assurances I had received from the young lady who wrote to me about employment were fulfilled, though the work was temporary. Later I obtained more promising employment in that situation and what with that and the dissatisfaction with my accommodation, we decided in the year 1903 to marry. We rented a single room in a tenement in the Govanhill district of Glasgow, a rather more respectable district than Gorbals, although for Parliamentary purposes Govanhill was included in the Gorbals constituency, then known as the Hutchesontown and Blackfriars Division. Our finances were anything but favourable: perhaps the marriage was a calculated risk, even though my wife continued her employment, because not long after I was again unemployed for more than three months. Among my recollections is our first New Year together when we had not a penny piece and were compelled to pawn some of our belongings to obtain a decent meal on New Year's Eve. At that time there was no Unemployment Benefit, no dole. One had to depend on borrowing or pawning one's household goods and sometimes had almost to starve.

I was extremely fortunate in my wife; a lovely person; very good-looking; beautiful features, vivacious, a wonderful dancer. She was in the tailoring trade, but with her fine voice and dancing, had appeared in several Glasgow pantomimes and concerts. Possibly, if she had not married me, she would have become a star. Later, when in more regular employment and settled in the Fairfield district of Glasgow, I began to receive some notice from the Press and we were able to entertain. Then she was the life and soul of every party. I had met her at a dance, where, however, we did no more than say 'how-do-you-do'. Later, when I was working in a workshop near Candleriggs, I saw her on her way to work. This happened on several occasions so I took the opportunity of speaking to her: as a result she introduced me to her family who, at that time, were living in the Gorbals district. Her father was ill and retired. Her mother, though far from well, was very active in the household; she had several sisters, and two brothers both associated with the bookmaking fraternity, one of whom had an excellent voice and was described as Scotland's favourite singer of coster songs. His name was Archie Freedman. His son, of the same name, was for many years Editor of the Scottish *Sunday Express*. Probably my appearances at the Speakers' Forum and association with one of the trade unions at that time may have accounted partly for my wife's family's coolness towards me, indicating perhaps that I was not one of them. Moreover, at the time I was engaged in a factory at no more than thirty shillings a week. Despite the disfavour of the family, although not too vigorously expressed, we decided to marry, a risk fraught with many, far too many, problems, but the start of fifty-one years of marital happiness.

By this time my father had returned from Shields to Glasgow. As usual he had quarrelled with those who employed him, and the agreement he had with the South Shields clothing firm was terminated. When he learned about my marriage he was furious and despite the hardship of our existence, we never went near him to ask for help. I learned that his anger was increased because of my Socialist views; although he had involved himself years before in London with efforts to form an organisation to protect the workers in the clothing trade he had no political views at all and, in fact, only voted Labour for the first time when I became a Member of Parliament many years afterwards. He was hardly interested when my first child, a daughter, was born but when a son came and we named him after father, that helped. By this time he was much more prosperous and, although in those days he was never happy about my activities, we were at last received in his home as though nothing had happened. My mother, bless her, must have urged him. Unfortunately, my employment was intermittent; I was in and out of work again and life was anything but pleasant. How we managed I often wonder.

Those who now get Unemployment Benefit and Supplementary Allowance cannot realise what working-class conditions were in the early part of this century. It was not until the Liberal Government was in office in 1908 that insurance schemes against unemployment and sickness came into operation, and even then the benefits were hardly enough to keep body and soul together. The Old Age Pension was fixed at five shillings a week and was subject to a means test. And there was no National Health Service. The usual doctor's fee varied from a shilling if one paid him a visit to two and six if he called. I don't suppose doctors who operated in working-class districts were well off; often bills were left unpaid.

At about this time we moved to the West End of Glasgow, where I had obtained employment. Not far from where we lived a murder had taken place and a man named Oscar Slater was arrested and charged with the offence. After his trial he was found guilty, but because there were grave doubts about the verdict, he was reprieved and sentenced to life imprisonment. Year after year petitions were sent to the various Home Secretaries in different governments demanding a re-trial, but they were always refused. I recall how Sir Arthur Conan Doyle, the author of the Sherlock Holmes series, after personal enquiry into the crime, came to the conclusion that Slater was convicted on the most flimsy circumstantial evidence, and that the Glasgow police exploited Slater's reputation as a professional gambler unfairly. Slater actually served eighteen years in Peterhead prison and then was pardoned. Few people in the neighbourhood believed he was guilty. Eventually the authorities came to the same conclusion, but supposing he had been hanged instead of being reprieved? An innocent man would have suffered the dread penalty of execution. The circumstances surrounding his trial and sentence caused me to turn my mind in the direction of abolition of capital punishment.

The first General Election in which I played a part occurred in 1906 when George Barnes, the Engineers' Secretary, contested the Gorbals Division of Glasgow against Bonar Law. The latter was a Canadian businessman, a friend of Max Aitken, later Lord Beaverbrook, and a protégé of the famous statesman, Joseph Chamberlain. Law had won the seat in the election of 1900 and was now defeated by Barnes. It was the first Labour victory in Scotland. I managed to get into the hall which at one time had been a boxing stadium, so I knew something about it. I listened to Bonar Law who was speaking about the need for tariff reform and was gaining considerable applause from what was obviously a Gorbals working-class audience.

After a while I could endure it no longer and rose to my feet and shouted, 'What about the workers?' It was a way of protesting when listening to political opponents who used arguments and stated policies which failed to appreciate the importance of those interests which affected the working class. One of the stewards came over and told me to stop, but later I was tempted to interrupt again, and this time the steward got hold of me by the jacket, dragged me to the stairs and practically threw me down.

I was long regarded as one of the Clydesiders, and referred to sometimes quite wrongly as one of the 'Wild men of the Clyde'. It was because of my general activities in Glasgow and the surrounding district that I have always been included among the Clydesiders, although frequently in dispute with them on matters of policy and activities, and though I did not represent a Glasgow constituency.

Several years later, when there was violent controversy in the ranks of Labour over the expulsion of Victor Grayson, who at the time was the Member of Parliament for Colne Valley and who had defied Keir Hardie, the Leader of the Party in the House of Commons, George Barnes was due to speak in a Glasgow theatre under the auspices of the Clarion Scouts. I had spoken in the place more than once myself, and decided to go to the meeting and face Barnes, who at the time was known to be opposed to Grayson. At the theatre door two stewards refused to allow me in. 'You stop out,' they said, 'we don't want any trouble.' However, I knew the place pretty well and went round to the stage door. There was nobody there and I made my way to a box on the ground floor, keeping my head down in order to escape notice. The Chairman and George Barnes duly arrived on the platform; Barnes was introduced and spoke quietly for about five minutes. Then he proceeded to make a vicious attack on Grayson. This was too much for me and I rose from my hiding place and did exactly what I had done at the Tory meeting several years before, when Barnes was contesting the 1906 Election in the Gorbals Division. Whatever I shouted out I cannot recall, but it was not long before a couple of stewards came to the box and dragged me out. So I had the experience of being ejected from a meeting where I supported Barnes and also from one when I was supporting Grayson against him. Some years later I became very friendly with Barnes; he was one of the ablest of Labour's political figures in those days and became a member of the War Cabinet when Lloyd George was Prime Minister.

The story of Victor Grayson is a strange one and contains a mystery which is unresolved to this day. Here are the details as I know them.

In 1907 there was a by-election in Colne Valley. The National Council of the Independent Labour Party decided to contest the Division and a number of names were suggested, mainly of leading members of the Party. Meanwhile, the local branch, fascinated by speeches Grayson had been making and his efforts on behalf of the unemployed in Manchester, decided that he should be the candidate. There was nothing the National Council of the ILP could do to prevent it. The ILP sponsored candidates until the '30s, and although the Labour Party was in existence, it had no power to overrule the local Party. Thus Grayson entered the lists and was successful. He was no politician, rather more of a propagandist and undoubtedly a most successful one, but he never succeeded in conforming to Parliamentary procedure. Moreover, he caused some disruption in the Parliamentary Labour Party by adopting an independent attitude which, however, gained him support from Robert Blatchford and H.M. Hyndman despite opposition from Hardie, MacDonald and Snowden. Eventually, defying Hardie's leadership, he was expelled and, when no longer an MP, engaged in a series of lectures which gave him a more or less satisfactory living until, at the outbreak of war, having been provided with funds by some friends, he emigrated to New Zealand and later joined the Australian Army. Some years later he returned to the UK. Setting out on a journey to join some friends, he failed to arrive and, from then, mysteriously vanished. Several efforts to write up the story about Grayson have been attempted, but the mystery of his disappearance has not been cleared up, and nothing has been published.

When I was attending the 1979 Labour Conference at Brighton I was approached by a lady named Mrs Watkins, who asked whether she could come and talk to me about Victor Grayson. I learned from her that she was Grayson's daughter, who had tried to have a book published about her father but without success. She asserted that he had been, within her knowledge, living with a lady in London who was — according to her version — benevolently inclined, when one evening two men had arrived, and taken Grayson out, placed him in a car and from then onwards he had disappeared. She was of the opinion that he had either become associated with British Government Agents or had defected to some other country, presumably Russia. Most of what I was told appeared to be speculations, and it is doubtful if it will ever proceed beyond that.

After another period of unemployment I got a job with the Scottish Wholesale Co-operative Society in their Shieldhall factory, and went to live in the Fairfield area, where many of the shipyards were situated, in order to be close to my new employment. I now had steady work after many removals and upheavals. I had moved from one room in the Govanhill district of Glasgow and then, after my marriage and a period of unemployment which lasted nearly four months, occupied a furnished room in another area. Then I moved again to the North side of Glasgow in the Gallowgate area; again a single room with varying periods of employment, with my wife occasionally resuming her previous occupation as a tailoress, until it appeared that an addition to the family was a possibility. Arrangements for other accommodation then became essential and the circumstances were of such a character that for a few weeks my wife went to stay with her mother. By this time her father had passed away, and our eldest child, a daughter, was born. Not long afterwards, I got the Co-op job and a two-room flat in the Fairfield district.

There I also joined the local branch of the Independent Labour Party and engaged in most of its propaganda activities, holding regular meetings at street corners and in their hall on Sunday nights. I had achieved some success as an open air speaker and became quite popular with the crowds who attended. Then, in the year 1909, the Liberal Government introduced the Trade Board's Bill, which passed through Parliament rapidly. Winston Churchill was President of the Board of Trade and he accepted my nomination by the Glasgow Trades Council and my trade union as a member of the Board to help in improving the conditions of workers in what were described as 'sweated trades'.

My appointment as the representative of the Scottish clothing workers was not because I possessed much knowledge about the condition of home workers. It was an appointment made to satisfy the belief among garment workers across the border that their interests would be represented. Naturally I learned, while attending the Trade Board meetings, much about the conditions of home workers, which were deplorable. Some, I understand, hired sewing machines, but even with mechanical aid seldom earned more than four or five shillings a week. It was strange to discover that those who exploited home workers were mostly the very emigrants who had become master tailors. Because of those conditions public opinion was aroused and the Government was forced to take action. It is doubtful whether the operations of the Trade Boards, either affecting the clothing, furniture or any other trades, were beneficial. The Factory Acts, if they existed at all, were 'more honoured in the breach than in the observance'. Inspectors were few in number and the law was ignored.

So, for about two years, on behalf of the clothing workers, I travelled to London once a month, except during the holiday season, to attend meetings at Government expense. My visits to London brought me into association with several of the trade union leaders, who stayed at the small hotel we occupied. We paid seven and six for bed and breakfast, which was about all it was worth. My fee from the Government for attendance was one pound a day, and when the cost of meals was taken into account there was not much left, but it provided a little useful pocket money. It also gave me the opportunity of several visits to the House of Commons and, from a seat in the Gallery, I listened with intense interest to the debates.

My knowledge of Parliamentary procedure was limited and I could never understand why, when the Motion for the Adjournment of the House was moved, they went on debating. This seemed very odd to me and even more so did the contents of many speeches from both the Tory and Liberal MPs. To me, coming from Glasgow, where I had lived amidst the squalid consequences of unemployment and poverty, everything seemed so irrelevant, and I made much use of this fact on my return to Glasgow when taking part in debates in the Trades Council and also when on the propaganda platform. Nor did it encourage me at that time to become a Member of Parliament; I was content to be an agitator or, as I believed, a missionary preaching social justice and denouncing Capitalism and all its works. No doubt the experience was useful, and must have increased my enthusiasm for discussion and determination to change the face of society.

My work in the Co-operative factory I found dull. What made matters worse was my disappointment with the Co-operative Movement. I failed to understand why those employed in the Co-operative Movement were no better off in pay and working conditions than those in private employment. No doubt conditions have vastly improved since then. The manager of the factory where I worked was an ignorant bully. His attitude made me long to escape from what I regarded as petty tyranny. However, when the foreman of the section where I was working decided to leave I applied to the manager for the post. 'You are far too young', he said. That settled the matter. I was determined to escape as soon as possible.

5

Champion of the Seamen

The opportunity to escape came at the beginning of 1911 after two monotonous and miserable years in the factory. My wages in the Co-operative job were thirty-five shillings a week, hardly enough to keep a wife and two children in comfort. I earned a little extra by writing modest articles for Co-operative periodicals. I also helped the Scottish Legal Assurance Society in committees appointed to deal with pension administration and other functions. (This work continued even when I had found employment with the Seamen's Union.) We lived frugally. Before my marriage and after, for many years, I did not taste alcoholic drinks. I did smoke; not cigarettes but a pipe; the tobacco was usually supplied free by seamen for services rendered.

My work for the seamen came about in this way. Havelock Wilson, the seamen's leader, had called a strike of seamen and asked the Glasgow Trades Council for their assistance. Though Wilson was disliked — he had been expelled from the Labour Party — the Council agreed, so on their behalf I offered my services. Already many men had left their ships and were on strike. They gathered at the Mercantile Marine office in the Broomielaw, alongside the docks. My help, addressing meetings, was confined to several evenings because of my work in the factory, but during the Glasgow holidays I was free for two weeks. At that time holidays with pay was unknown, but I gave my services during the two holiday weeks and never asked for, or expected, any payment from the seamen.

Wilson was associated with the Labour Movement as far back as the '80s and became MP for Middlesbrough. His Union, the National Union of Seamen, was always in financial difficulties and he was in financial trouble, largely owing to a

45

legal action against a shipping company as a result of which he became bankrupt: there were also rumours about improper use of Union funds. However, although aware of his reputation we agreed to assist the seamen because of their shocking wages and working conditions.

On the Clyde, as in Liverpool and Southampton, the bulk of the shipping consisted of liners. From the Clyde every Saturday throughout the year at least three liners — one owned by the Anchor Line, another by the Allen Line and a third by the Donaldson Line — were crowded with emigrants leaving for America and Canada. The emigrants were seeking an escape from low wages and unemployment in the UK, and were optimistic about prospects in Canada, the USA, Australia and New Zealand. When I became national organiser of one of the seamen's unions I had occasion to witness in person the emotional scenes associated with those departures, and helped to console relatives of the emigrants. I had also to find replacements for crew absentees; 'pier head jumps' we called them. Some who had never been to sea were signed on, probably deserted on the other side; it was unusual for a liner to leave port without changes of crew below deck.

These Atlantic liners usually had a three-week voyage, ten days or so crossing the Atlantic, a few days at their destination, and ten or twelve days on the return. The men on deck were receiving, before the strike, four pounds monthly. Those below, firemen and trimmers, received four pounds ten shillings a month. A few men were engaged alongside the principal engineers in the engine room and received a few shillings more. The seamen demanded a minimum of five pounds for deck hands and five pounds ten shillings per month for the men who worked in the stokehold. This demand was rejected by the shipowners and was responsible for the strike.

I took part in the negotiations because the Union had no branch, only a small office. An empty shop was rented and a man was sent by Wilson to take charge. Our first task was to raise funds to provide some cash for the strikers. There was no strike pay. The Union had no funds but we were successful because of sympathy among the general public for the seamen. Then the dockers who were also at that time unorganised — they had belonged to a dockers' union with headquarters in

London, but had abandoned their membership because of the absence of benefits — came out in sympathy with the seamen, and I was asked to address meetings of the dockers in various parts of the Clyde, and occasionally at Leith and in Dundee. I also took part in negotiations with the shipowners, and we were able to obtain, though not without some difficulty, an assurance that the deck hands would receive what they had asked for, namely five pounds a month, and the stokehold men five pounds ten shillings. The men complained also about conditions on board ship, the poor accommodation and food, and the attitude of some ships' officers. It was essential occasionally to meet either the marine superintendent of a liner company or a director, and seek remedies which would satisfy the men. I maintained friendships for many years with ships' officers with whom I had negotiated almost daily for a time on some issue of concern both to deck hands and those working in the stokehold.

Some of the shipowners were ruthless and even unscrupulous, but others, a minority, were enlightened and inclined to be more generous. For example, the Chairman of the Allen Line, James Allen, who had become a member of the Independent Labour Party, and was described by the Press as the millionaire Socialist, and Algernon Henderson, Chairman of the Anchor Line and associated with the Cunard Line, were both sympathetic and willing to meet the men's demands. One well-known shipowner, not associated with the liner trade, named Maclay, who owned many cargo vessels, earned the name 'Holy Joe', and was alleged to present members of his crews at Christmas with a copy of the New Testament. (I have reason to believe his descendants are more generous.) I became friendly with Henderson, who was shocked by the number of people leaving Scotland due to poverty and unemployment, and discovered that he was interested in social reform. He asked my advice about books to read. Undoubtedly his attitude and the sympathetic support of the dockers contributed to our success.

Unfortunately, we learned that Havelock Wilson had reached an arrangement with the Shipping Federation, the supreme authority in the shipping industry, to accept a reduced increase of ten shillings monthly for deck hands and the same for men below deck. We also learned that this caused considerable discontent in Liverpool and in particular Southampton. Seamen in the latter port resigned from the National Union and formed another organisation, the British Seafarers' Union. We subsequently learned that Wilson had agreed with the Shipping Federation to accept the smaller sum on the understanding that employment would only be available to those who had joined his Union.

Wilson sent two of his colleagues to the Clyde with the intention of closing the branch because we had obtained a higher rate of pay. They were Dick McGhee, who was a Nationalist MP for an Irish constituency, and a Captain Tupper, who spread the story that he had been in the Army and had won the Victoria Cross. He had done nothing of the sort and was discovered later to be an impostor.

As a result of Wilson's decision to close the branch, it was decided to form the Scottish Seamen's Union, but meanwhile I was asked by the dockers to become their Secretary at a wage far in excess of anything I had previously received. I declined, because the Trades Council had sent me to help the seamen and not the dockers, and it might have been regarded as improper if I accepted the appointment. But I was offered the post of Secretary to the new Scottish Union at two pounds per week, which I accepted. At any rate it would offer an opportunity to escape from the drudgery of the Shieldhall factory, and there was a possibility of brighter prospects.

However, I had fallen from the frying pan into the fire. The experience was far from pleasant, not because of criticism by the seamen, with whom I was popular then and for many years afterwards, but owing to the action of Wilson who used every opportunity, legal and otherwise, to destroy the Scottish Union.

Unfortunately, the Trades Union Congress, on the instigation of Ernest Bevin who had formed the Transport Workers' Union, disliked anything in the nature of a breakaway Union and when, some time later, the Scottish Union and the British Seafarers of Southampton amalgamated with a Union representing the catering section of the seamen to form the Amalgamated Marine Workers' Union, and I became their National Organiser, the TUC sent a deputation consisting of their General Secretary, Fred Bramley, and Arthur Walkden, General

Secretary of one of the railwaymen's unions, and a man named Keen, who was the Secretary of a Birmingham Union, to propose ending the operations of our Union. They offered our General Secretary and his deputy and myself a thousand pounds each to resign as we were a thorn in the flesh of Havelock Wilson. Our General Secretary accepted, but the deputy and I refused. The language I used to Mr Bramley and the TUC is unrepeatable. Eventually, as a result of legal action, injunctions and nefarious activities indulged in by the Wilson gang, we were prevented from utilising our own funds until it was found impossible to continue operations.

My experiences during that period were more than exciting; I was threatened by thugs to stop me from addressing meetings, and on one occasion was fired at by one of Wilson's hired men, with the result that the person standing beside me was killed. Then, with the aid of skilled lawyers and the presence on the Bench of a Judge, Lord Anderson, who had been a Liberal MP and was a political appointment, the culprit was acquitted on grounds of self-defence, although nobody had sought to attack him, nor was there any evidence that he had suffered any injury.

However, I do admit that my association with the seamen evoked considerable criticism. I had never, apart from a few trips to Ireland and a voyage in a cargo ship as passenger, gone to sea. Yet I engaged in negotiations on behalf of the seamen with several shipping companies, and can claim some success. I experienced no difficulty in understanding what seamen required in working conditions and wages on Atlantic liners and tramp vessels and in the coastal trade. I also gained considerable knowledge, as a result of my intervention in the dispute, about industrial conditions in the docks; about casual labour and the shocking system of employment, all of considerable value to me when I was a Member of Parliament. Indeed, I had become almost an authority on shipping when I joined my Labour colleagues at Westminster. I shared in debates and was frequently asked for advice on shipping matters. Moreover, I gained in general knowledge of social and human affairs from my association with seamen, many of whom had sailed to remote places with frequent absences from home, on low wages and in the unsatisfactory conditions of seafaring life. Ironically, a few years later I was made Chairman of the Labour Party Shipping Group and in 1945 I was awarded an honorary life membership of the National Seamen's Union marked, 'For services rendered'.

I am proud to place on record what I owe to the seafarers, the mining community and those in HM Forces, and how my education benefited from my intervention in 1911 on behalf of the Glasgow Trades Council in the seamen's dispute.

It was fortunate from my point of view that as a result of joining a union early in my career I was sent as a delegate to the Glasgow Trades Council, at that time perhaps the most influential trade union organisation in Scotland. My association with that body began my real education in politics. The Trades Council at that time — it was formed back in the '80s of the last century — in the absence of a Central Labour Party in Glasgow, dealt not only with industrial topics, but with many political issues. The intrusion of politics was not always regarded with favour by the trade union members of the Council, but gradually the deliberations of the Council when dealing with demarcation problems, solving disputes between the unions, inevitably led to debates on social issues; pensions, the need for improved housing, and activities of governments, both Conservative and Liberal, which, under pressure, had been forced to introduce limited measures of social reform. Therefore, under the influence of Blatchford's *Clarion* and his other writings, the debates at the Glasgow Trades Council meetings and subsequently joining the Independent Labour Party, I was induced to become a member of Blatchford's Clarion Scouts. I became a member of its Speakers' Class where we were taught to speak. Many of those who joined it no doubt required to be taught, but as it happened I required no tuition, even if what I said was regarded by those who listened as a load of rubbish.

I confess that without formal schooling, to gain knowledge in those subjects which are the essential ingredients of political understanding is a formidable undertaking. However, I gained by frequent attendance at the Speakers' Forum at Glasgow Green, to which reference has been made, but should recall an incident which contributed to my knowledge following a discussion I had with someone in the presence of a small group of people. I used a word which I was convinced was correctly pronounced, only to be rebuked by my opponent, a response which I resented, but on my next visit to the Forum I was presented by the same person with a dictionary, accompanied by a remark, 'I hope this will satisfy you.' I found it of substantial interest and assistance. Let me confess, I still avail myself of a dictionary. I am bound to add as part of my education, not only the animated discussions at the Glasgow Trades Council and with my colleagues of the Independent Labour Party, but also the heckling to which I was frequently subjected by those who appeared to have a knowledge superior to my own. Incidentally, I would dare say that Scottish hecklers are more politically conscious and aggressive than any others I have met, perhaps with the exception of the Welsh who, however, are more polite.

I regard my association with the Glasgow Trades Council from 1903, when I became a delegate from my trade union branch until my membership of the House of Commons in 1922, as a most valuable contribution to my social and industrial education. During the later years of the last century and the early years of the present century Trades Councils in most industrial centres exercised considerable influence. They consisted of delegates from trade union branches where many political and related subjects were discussed; Socialist organisations like the Independent Labour Party, the Fabian Society and the Social Democratic Federation then existed and were permitted to attend and participate in debates, though most trade union branches objected to political intervention.

The Council of the Trades Union Congress, unlike the Scottish Congress, was strongly opposed to the operations of Trades Councils, who were regarded as exercising too much influence, encouraging political discussion and, consequently, were considered to be an obstacle to trade union membership. It was not until the Labour Party was fully established and responsible for policy and Parliamentary representation in 1918 that the Trades Councils began to lose their influence, and in their original form gradually faded away. In Glasgow, for example, there was no central organisation of the Labour Party when in 1906 the Parliamentary Labour Party was first formed, so the Glasgow Trades Council, responsible for industrial affairs, continued its political activities and remained the most influential organisation in Glasgow and West of Scotland Labour and Trade Union Movement.

I recall how I looked forward with interest and even excitement to the regular Wednesday night meetings which took place in one of the city halls attended by two hundred and fifty and sometimes four hundred members, depending on the subjects to be debated. The debates were exciting and informative and it was remarkable that the local Press, even newspapers like the *Glasgow Herald* and the *Scotsman*, devoted more attention to the proceedings of the Trades Council than to the Glasgow Town Council and other local authorities. My name and comment on our activities were seldom absent from the newspapers, whose circulation covered not only Scotland but even crossed the border, though criticism of my speeches was inevitable. I realised, even then, that to have my name appearing in the Press, however adverse the criticism, was of some consequence. Therefore, though I declare truthfully that without any ambition to become an MP, my membership of the Glasgow Trades Council, the trade union, association with the seafaring community, including my perhaps swashbuckling speeches at street corners and park gates, and general activities, made it not altogether surprising that my name was mentioned as a possible candidate for a Parliamentary constituency.

I probably made more progress and gained more knowledge through the medium of the Trades Council than elsewhere. Beginning as a delegate I became Vice-Chairman, then President, following which I became the representative of the Council on the Scottish Trade Union Congress and, until 1908, the Scottish Labour Party, and in 1920 I became the fraternal delegate of the Scottish Trade Union Congress to the Irish Trade Union Congress at Cork. I reckon that what I gained in knowledge of industrial relations, the problems facing the trade unions because of adverse legislation impeding their progress, and sharing influence with fellow members of the various organisations, was of greater value than reading a library of books on related subjects. Moreover, apart from debates on industrial issues we frequently debated foreign affairs and policy on social problems of local and national interest. As the Council was also responsible for the selection of candidates for the Town Council, I was appointed to fight a seat in an exclusively working-class district in 1912, but without success. Before the First World War the Labour Movement met with greater success in mixed communities than in those affected by excessive unemployment and poverty. Then, in 1916, I became a member of the Glasgow Town Council representing the ship-building area of Fairfield. My principal supporters consisted of skilled shipwrights and engineers.

Popular as I became because of my public speeches, some prominent colleagues in the Town Council sought to oppose my election. They preferred to pursue a moderate policy, which induced me to ask sometimes awkward questions, usually taking my own line. I recall one of the old members when I arrived in the Council Chambers advising me not to speak for at least three months. 'They don't like it,' he said. I was only there three days when I made a speech attacking the Council for their complacency on housing and transport needs, which gained me considerable support — not in the Council, but among the public. Before long I appeared to have made myself, in the opinion of some colleagues, something of a nuisance and, in consequence, the leader of the Labour Group in the Council, John Wheatley, an exceedingly able politician and businessman who later became a member of the Cabinet in the first Labour Government, threatened my expulsion from the Party. This would have increased my popularity. However, they failed.

In the course of my frequent interventions as a member of the Glasgow Town Council and the West of Scotland Trade Union Movement — some may be inclined to assert they were much too numerous — my main concern, apart from the existing and growing unemployment problem, the necessity of promoting legislation to raise the standard of living and my vision of a civilised society was, before the First World War and for many years afterwards, primarily the pay and conditions of those who were associated with the Merchant Navy.

It was customary, after a member of the Council had three years' service, to be appointed Junior Baillie, the equivalent in Scotland of Magistrate, but there was no such appointment for me. Even after serving an additional three years when a member should be appointed Senior Baillie and to a position on the Licensing Bench as well as ordinary Police Court, I was again rejected. However, as I succeeded in gaining the Parliamentary constituency of Linlithgow in 1922, and after my success visited the Town Council and stated my intention to confine my activities to Parliament and resign from the Council, I was the recipient of cordial congratulations from the self-same members who had refused to appoint me as a Magistrate. So I failed in what was my ambition; inspired after all only by the desire to occupy the Bench instead of the dock where I had to appear on several occasions, not for picking pockets or anything fraudulent, but simply because when I held meetings in various parts of Glasgow I was often charged with obstruction. Any meeting where Socialism or the policy of the Labour Movement was advocated was regarded as subversive and prohibited. Imagine my disappointment! Honours galore: Privy Councillor, Cabinet Minister, Minister of Fuel and Power, Secretary for War, Minister of Defence, Chairman of the Parliamentary Labour Party, Companion of Honour, D.C.L. Durham, LL.D. Sussex, Hon. Fellow of Sunderland Polytechnic, President of the Easington Council of Voluntary Service, President of the World Sporting Club, London, Freeman of the City of London and many others, yet never made a JP or a Glasgow Baillie! No justice in this world! Still, one can't expect to have everything.

From 1906 onwards there was considerable disquiet in political circles and the Liberal Government about the possibility of conflict with Germany and when, after negotiations had broken down, it was eventually decided to prepare for war, it was obvious that Great Britain was far from ready. Before 1914 when war became inevitable, the Navy League was demanding the construction of a number of battleships. Their slogan was 'We won't wait. We want eight,' by which they meant that no fewer than eight huge battleships were essential if we were involved in war. As it happened the absence of sufficient battleships of the kind demanded by the Navy League gave me the opportunity, because of my official connection with the Seamen's Union, to undertake certain duties on behalf of both the Admiralty and the newly created Ministry of Shipping.

Many Atlantic liners were taken over by the Admiralty and converted into auxiliary vessels with limited armament. At that time, of course, they were powered by coal, not oil, and consequently a vast number of men were required for the stokehold as firemen and for the engine room. They were difficult to obtain because many had joined the Forces or were needed on munition production. Many seafarers were reluctant to join auxiliary vessels with limited armament; they did not ensure sufficient protection. In the first few months of war hundreds of our vessels were torpedoed and thousands of lives were lost.

However, on Government instructions, I succeeded in collecting men from the Clyde, Leith Docks, Dundee and elsewhere throughout Scotland, in particular the Western Highlands, who were prevailed upon, on the assurance of higher wages than the average seaman received, to accept employment on auxiliary vessels. My function was to collect them, transfer them to one of the stations, then to London, transport them to Southampton where most of the liners were located, and get them aboard. This, perhaps, seems easy; in fact, it was more difficult than being at the Front, because my recruits always received an advance, before sailing, of at least a third of the pay to which they would be entitled at the end of a voyage. Most of the available funds were expended in liquor, so that it was with the utmost difficulty that I could get the men first of all aboard the trains in Glasgow, Leith Docks and elsewhere, and eventually aboard ship in Southampton. I had to control them by firmness and also, occasionally, by dealing physically with the difficult ones. Looking back, I have often wondered how I managed; it was not courage, but just that a job had to be done.

Between 1909 and 1914 the country was in a condition of industrial crisis, because of a series of disputes which were the most disturbing in my experience. Engineers, shipbuilders, miners, transport workers and seamen went on strike and it is possible that without the outbreak of war something close to revolution might have occurred. Certainly the Liberal Government, described as a Government of all the talents, would have encountered serious trouble.

Despite Union activities mainly associated with looking after the interests of seamen, I undertook commitments as a member of the Glasgow Trades Council and of the Independent Labour Party. I was concerned with several disputes caused by the attitude of somewhat unscrupulous landlords who took advantage of the absence of servicemen to force their wives to pay increased rent. This was brought to the attention of the Trades

Council who decided that the workers should be called upon to assist their comrades in the Forces and their families at home by refusing to pay the rents demanded. I was one of those who, although able to pay the increase, went on strike with the others and refused to pay my rent. I had to prove to rent strikers that I was as sincere as they were in protest against such deplorable action.

We also had trouble with school authorities who, for some reason, decided that parents would have to pay for their children's school books. It was customary in Glasgow and no doubt elsewhere in the country to provide free books, some even of a technical character, for children, many of whom possessed the ability to enter the higher scholastic institutions. We decided that parents should refuse to pay for books; the Education Authorities must accept responsibility. This was another strike in which I was involved. I was almost the last person to yield and was summoned to appear before the Court and fined one pound.

Because of such activities I became fairly prominent; at any rate my name appeared in the newspapers. Thus it was suggested that I might become a candidate for Parliament at the next General Election. At the time I had no such ambition, but when an invitation came from a constituency not on the Clyde, but from the County of Linlithgow — otherwise known as West Lothian — I agreed with some reluctance to attend a Selection Conference. Another candidate for selection was the popular local miners' leader, Hugh Murnin, but to my surprise I gained a majority vote and thus became the Labour candidate for West Lothian. No doubt my activities had helped.

No one can escape harsh criticism in politics; I have received full measure without complaining. But I have some little resentment because of the accusation, mostly suggested anonymously but sometimes in the public Press, that I was a conscientious objector in the First World War. Nothing could be further from the truth. I was engaged on work of national importance on behalf of shipping: mine was therefore officially a reserved occupation.

Here I place on record my sincere regard and admiration for those who hold genuine convictions in their advocacy of peace and pacifism, though unable to agree with them. Whatever is said or thought to the contrary, even if one is accused of being chauvinist, it is, in my judgement, the responsibility of every person to seek by whatever means are at his or her disposal to contribute to the nation's security. I am no warmonger. Peace, universal peace, is as much my objective as it is of any confirmed pacifist. My purpose is not to provoke war, but to deter it. We must promote our defensive strength consistent with our financial capabilities so that a potential aggressor should realise that nothing is to be gained by aggression; but negotiation, discussion, understanding and, wherever possible, consensus should be the objective rather than confrontation.

When the war ended in 1918 with victory for Great Britain and her allies, Lloyd George, who had become Prime Minister in 1916, decided to form a Coalition Government. He had made advances to the leaders of the Conservative Party during the war, and though most Conservatives were distrustful, they eventually agreed to join his Coalition. I stood for the first time in that Election and gained a considerable Labour vote. In fact, my vote was the highest for Labour in any County Division in Scotland. But I was defeated all the same. What a contest it was! I had no trade union backing, hardly any money, one old broken-down car, but many loyal friends.

I remained a candidate for this Parliamentary constituency, and devoted attention to it, making myself familiar with conditions and aspirations of the electors, along with other activities as member of the Glasgow Town Council and the Trades Council. There is one example which I always remember with satisfaction; I would not say that about all my activities, sometimes undertaken without regard to the sentiments of colleagues; but the incident to which I now refer is one about which I can feel proud.

It came to my knowledge that the men and women who worked in the Glasgow Asylum for the Blind, themselves sightless, were being treated in a fashion which one would not expect to exist in what was, after all, a charitable institution. It was alleged that the Manager — or Chief Director — was a tyrant; that the conditions as regards payment, hours of labour and social needs of those blind persons were not brought to the notice of either the public or even subscribers to the Institution. A delegation of three blind persons approached me and asked if

I could render them some assistance. I had no idea how to help, but they mentioned that complaints might be raised at the Annual Meeting of the Institution and that I should become a subscriber, which required the payment of one guinea a year. They went further by suggesting they would provide the guinea. Accordingly I sent my donation, became a full subscribing member and attended the first Annual Meeting. The Chairman made the familiar speech, expressing sympathy with the afflicted, assuring the subscribers that the best attention was given to those who worked for the Institution, and his remarks were received with approbation by most of the subscribers present. He was about to close the proceedings when I rose to ask a question. He tried to brush me aside, but apparently was not aware of the sort of person I am. I didn't like being brushed aside and made that immediately clear. I wanted to know why the Director had refused to meet a delegation of the blind persons to discuss their conditions. Again he sought to terminate the proceedings and gained the consent of what he described as the majority of those present. That was my first attempt.

I must here admit to a characteristic — I would not call it a quality — which has sometimes evoked trouble. I am reluctant to enter into a quarrel or any activity suggested to me, but once convinced that action is required because of the moral principle involved, my hesitation disappears. But if I am to take part I must do it with all the intensity in my possession. Call it courage, or vanity, or stupidity, I simply can't help it. Furthermore, I can't tolerate anything which appears to be unjust. So we waited for the next Annual Meeting, by which time I had organised something of an opposition. I obtained the support of a well-known lawyer who was known to have radical sympathies, although not a member of the Labour Party, and my intentions were endorsed by colleagues on the Town Council. A few of us gathered before the next Annual Meeting of the Asylum and decided that on this occasion whoever was Chairman would be forced to take notice of our complaints. Again we had the familiar proceedings; a short optimistic speech from the Chair, the usual applause from the subscribers, a statement of accounts and the decision of the Chair to bring the proceedings to an end. Then we struck, by demanding that the complaints of some of the sightless people whom we had brought with us should be heard. There was a terrific rumpus and, in some parts of the hall, almost a scuffle, which led to police intervention. At first sight this would have seemed to be a complete defeat for us, but the newspapers the following day gave a full report of the proceedings, and for the first time since the Institution had been created questions were asked about the conditions that existed there. I had the satisfaction of learning not long afterwards that wages and conditions had improved, and the sightless people — although they had not obtained all they had asked for — were overjoyed that the tyranny to which they had been subjected had been completely removed. If I cannot claim any other achievement, this will suffice.

6

Arrested and Jailed

A campaign in which I took a prominent part a little later proved much more dramatic, and resulted for me in a much more drastic conflict with the law.

In 1919 the Clyde Workers' Committee, formed during the First World War to safeguard the interests of munition workers, approached the Glasgow Trades Council, of which at the time I was president, and requested the Council to help procure a reduction in the hours of labour in order to absorb the unemployed. A vast number who had been demobilised from the Forces, were unable to find employment. The average hours of labour in the shipyards, engineering and other industrial establishments were about fifty-six and in some industries round about sixty. There was no five-day-week policy operating at the time.

The Trades Council decided that two members should meet the Clyde Workers' Committee to discuss working hours. I was one of those selected. At the meeting, I listened to the demand for a reduction to a thirty-hour week, which I regarded as excessive, and suggested it would be more realistic to suggest a reduction of hours to forty per week. Despite opposition my proposition was accepted.

The question then arose of forming a committee to organise demonstrations, and I was proposed as its Chairman. I declined at first but, because of the unanimous demand at the meeting, I reluctantly agreed.

We held meetings in various parts of Glasgow and in some of the neighbouring towns, like Coatbridge, Airdrie, Motherwell, etc., and most prominent members of the Labour Party rendered assistance, though we knew that some of those associated with the Clyde Workers' Committee were inclined to advocate their revolutionary objectives. The official unions were opposed.

After a series of demonstrations which got us nowhere — the Government paid no attention — it was decided that a demonstration should be organised to meet in George Square in the city centre, and that a delegation should interview the Lord Provost in the Municipal Chambers, and ask him to intercede with Lloyd George, the Prime Minister, on our behalf. I was a member of the Town Council, and had access to the City Chambers. The demonstration was called for a Friday and practically the whole of the Square in front of the Municipal Buildings was filled: probably eighty thousand people were there. Among my colleagues were David Kirkwood — himself a Town Councillor — and William Gallacher, who was a member of the Communist Party. No speeches were made, but it was decided that Kirkwood and myself should enter the Municipal Buildings and see the Lord Provost, leaving Gallacher in charge, with strict instructions to maintain order. The Lord Provost was disinclined even to listen to us. His view was that this was a matter for the Government. Meanwhile, while we were engaged in discussion, it appeared that a tramcar was making its way through a part of the Square to the annoyance of some of the demonstrators. There was something of a scuffle. Unable to get anything useful from the Lord Provost, Kirkwood and I left the building.

We had only been a few minutes in the building, but by this time hundreds of police were in sight and began to use their batons in brutal fashion. Unfortunately, some of the crowd were forced up one of the side streets in trying to escape from the Square, and there happened to be a lorry stacked with empty bottles which they began to hurl at the police. The demonstrators were incensed at the attitude of the police, who were using their batons against people who had committed no offence.

During my public life I have seldom, if ever, been critical of the police; they have a duty to perform. In my experience they have proved their worth, but the action of some during the demonstration in George Square was deplorable. I don't suggest that all members of the Police Force were brutal, but am convinced many were, in particular those who were recruited from the Western Highlands and Islands; they had, to quote a familiar saying 'heather growing in their ears'. They seemed to have a grievance against Glasgow people.

Within a few minutes the Sheriff appeared at the corner of the Municipal Building and read the Riot Act. We were not aware of what had happened to require his presence, but learned later that a Labour Member of the Government named Roberts had told the Prime Minister that he thought the demonstration was intended to start a revolution. It was only eighteen months after the 1917 revolution in Russia, and undoubtedly there was a climate of opinion — not confined or peculiar to the Clyde, but almost over the whole country— that the Russians should be supported because they had destroyed Czarism. Indeed, at the end of 1917, immediately after the revolution, a conference by the Labour Movement had been held in Leeds with almost every prominent Labour politician and trade union leader present, including men like Ernest Bevin and Philip Snowden. They both made speeches; so did I. When they passed the resolution congratulating Lenin, Trotsky and their colleagues on their achievement, they expressed the reservation that the revolution would benefit Russia. There was no demand for a British revolution.

Why was it that the Sheriff appeared so readily? Why were hundreds of police available within seconds of the tramcar incident? What is even more important, if there was any incitement or intention to riot, why, when twelve persons including myself were arrested and accused of incitement to riot, was no evidence to that effect adduced at our trial in the Court of Session in Edinburgh? Incitement to riot was certainly never the purpose of the demonstrators; nor was it the intention of David Kirkwood, myself and others. Nor, so far as I was aware, was it the intention of William Gallacher. Our sole purpose was to persuade the Lord Provost to request the Prime Minister to introduce legislation, if at all possible, to reduce hours of labour and to enable unemployed people, the majority of whom were ex-servicemen, to be gainfully employed.

Not only was there an absence of evidence at the Court of Sessions to justify the accusation of rioting or inciting to riot, but Lord Scott Dickson, the presiding judge, acquitted ten of the twelve accused and expressed his doubts about any threat of revolution, or even incitement to riot, by sending Gallacher, the Communist, to prison for only three months and myself, who had advocated in lenient terms the moderate change of forty hours instead of thirty hours, he sentenced to five months, perhaps because I was Chairman of the Committee. The fact is that the Government were pleased to have some industrial trouble as a cover-up for their egregious blunders in failing to promote beneficial legislation which might favour those who were unemployed. The lavish promises during the war about 'a land fit to live in' were forgotten.

There is an additional factor. In 1916 Lloyd George was asked to visit Glasgow to meet the munition workers and discuss a proposal that the unskilled workers should work alongside skilled artisans and receive similar payment, which would have had the effect of eroding the wages of skilled engineers. At first Lloyd George refused to appear, but eventually, under pressure, agreed to speak in St Andrew's Hall in Glasgow before a packed audience of munition workers who were in favour of increased production of munitions and only demanded recognition of their skill. Instead of an assurance of consideration he treated them with scorn and talked with his customary eloquence of creating after the war 'a land fit for heroes'. As might be expected they shouted him down. He got his revenge in 1919.

When I left the City Chambers the police had succeeded in dividing the crowd, so I found a gap and stood on a seat and tried, by raising my voice, to persuade people to leave the Square. A few friends who were there suggested I should go to the Trades Council office nearby and complain. Nobody tried to prevent me and when I entered our office I found Willie Shaw, our Secretary, destroying some papers, and asked what he was doing. He said that during our discussions some of the Communist members had made fantastic suggestions about how to frighten the Government and he decided to burn anything subversive they had written. Soon after Pat Dollan, Town Councillor and my close friend, and others arrived, and it was decided to hold a meeting at the YMCA hall in Bothwell Street to consider what action to take. No decision was reached and the most sensible action was to go home, which I did. About one-thirty in the morning there was a knock at my door and several policemen came in; one said, 'We have come to arrest you'. I made no protest and, having consoled my wife, went to the only other room to say goodbye to my two children. The police followed me, and took me downstairs, where I saw almost a dozen policemen. I was taken to the local police station and placed in a cell with no furniture of any kind, not even a seat, so I lay on the floor and went off to sleep; I had been under some stress during the activities connected with the trouble and was tired out. The only person who spoke to me was a detective who said, 'You will get five years for this.' I asked him what for. 'For rioting,' he said, and I almost laughed in his face.

I was sent to Calton gaol in Edinburgh; one of the oldest and most squalid prisons in the country. I expected to be treated as a political prisoner but, said the ex-military Governor, 'There is no such thing in Scotland.' The food was abominable so, apart from some bread, I refused to eat it and was brought before the doctor, who insisted that the food was excellent; to which I responded that he could eat it himself. From both the prison doctor and the Governor the treatment was most unfavourable and objectionable. I never made any complaint about the Chief Warder and his colleagues; by them I was treated with the utmost consideration. No privileges, of course; no extra food. I practically lived on either the horrible porridge or bread throughout the whole of my prison sentence; I must, however, admit that I was much healthier on my release than on my entry. If I have any complaint to make it is that I was forced to leave my notebook behind; for what reason I could never understand. I had made no criticism of the prison or the Governor or of anybody. I had even made an effort to write some poetry.

It was discovered that some of the trade unions and Labour organisations in Edinburgh where the Calton Prison was situated were holding demonstrations outside the prison, demanding my release and asserting that I was a victim of a political manoeuvre for which Lloyd George was responsible. As a result for the first six or seven weeks I was not permitted to leave my cell; the only possible reason being that the authorities feared the demonstrations might possibly lead to a revolution — only eighteen months after the revolution in Russia! But one day I received a visitor, Dr Devon, who was a Prison Commissioner with whom I had become acquainted some years before when he attended a function associated with the Glasgow Town Council, of which I was a member. Following his intervention, the next day I was permitted to leave my cell and was taken down to the ash pit, and for several days afterwards my function was to collect useful cinders, presumably because of the economic situation of the country following the Great War.

On another occasion I was asked to follow one of the warders into the prison garden; much more pleasant than remaining in my cell or working at the ash pit. Though warders, according to the rules, were not permitted to engage in conversation with prisoners the warder seemed to be interested in the rose garden, and told me that he grew roses himself. I asked him whether he intended to remain a prison warder. 'By no means,' he said. 'I am hoping for another job.' 'What is that?' I asked. He said, 'I understand the prison hangman is talking about retiring. I would like to have his job.' Lyrical about roses, and an ambition to be a hangman!

There was a library in the prison which consisted of two cells. The warder librarian would sometimes take me down to this so-called library where I could select books. There was a remarkable variety of books which apparently people would send to the prison, among them I found Shelley's Prose Works which, so far as I knew, was unobtainable outside. The warder was, I regret to say, almost illiterate. If one asked for a book he would reply, 'Oh yes, I know what you want. It's by Watty Scott.' Evidently the only author he had ever heard of was Sir Walter.

I have no hesitation in saying that what happened in George Square on that Friday, the presence of the police and the tanks in the street and soldiers on the roof tops, and the attitude of the police to those who were committing no offence, was a deliberate act on the part of Lloyd George. Our sole compensation was the attitude of the judge who seemed to understand our objective. Perhaps, though our purpose was beyond reproach, some of my speeches were disliked. It may strike many people as somewhat remarkable that sixty years after the demand on the Clyde and other industrial centres for a reduction in the hours of labour as an approach to the solution of the unemployment problem, it is now demanded by the official trade unions and all

65

the prominent trade union leaders, whose forebears in the Trade Union Movement treated us in 1919 with severe condemnation.

The events associated with what was known as the Forty Hours Strike, regarded by Lloyd George, though not by every member of his Government, as the beginning of revolution, was on the contrary none other than a constitutional effort, by means of demonstrations, to draw attention to the need for shortening the hours of labour in order to absorb the unemployed, vast numbers of whom had returned from the Forces. On those occasions, far from friends deserting me, I found myself becoming extremely popular, excepting perhaps in the Press. The Glasgow Trades Council presented me with a gold watch. I was the recipient of scores of letters, congratulating me on my release, also on my activities on behalf of seamen, and in the Glasgow Town Council. Most pleasant of all was the request from the West Lothian Labour Party that I should again become their candidate for Parliament at the next election. As I shall explain in more detail, I was their candidate in 1918 though defeated in a straight fight by the existing Tory MP who had joined the Lloyd George Coalition, and again became their candidate in 1922 when I was to win the seat. Any resentment expressed at the time about my activities and conviction with the forty hours affair came, as I have said, from the Press, about which it is pointless to make complaint. I would not have expected them to do other than criticise somebody who, in the opinion of the redoubtable Lloyd George, was bent on revolution. When I recall my efforts to promote a realistic policy first on the ILP and the trade union movement, in particular my moderation in the forty hours affair, I can only regard the vindictive references in the Press as ironical. Though often frustrated by the sluggish groaning of the Parliamentary system I have never accepted revolution or extremism as the solution of our social problems.

My family stood by me throughout my imprisonment. They had a hard time. All I was able to obtain for my wife and two children was an allowance of a pound a week from my union. As a result my wife, for most of the time, obtained work outside the household. On my release from prison I found I was heavily in debt: bills had piled up. I had difficulty with shipowners because I had asked my members to engage in a dispute in which they were not involved. I sacrificed my position and encountered many difficulties for what I regarded as a principle. I made many opponents and even enemies, but gained many friends.

7

From 'Red Clyde' to Westminster

The years between 1918 and 1922 were an exciting and significant period in the political history of our country. The war was over, the nation was elated with victory, euphoria spread throughout the towns and cities of Britain like a hurricane. The slogans of prominent members of the Government were optimistic. Sir Eric Geddes, who was Secretary for War during the conflict, declared that 'we would squeeze the pips out of the Germans', and Lloyd George added, 'We will pick it all out of their pockets.'

The period was also a watershed, marking the declining supremacy of the established political parties and the emergence of a Radical Movement, whose hard core was the trade unions allied with the Labour Party. Lloyd George was responsible for an outrageous blunder. He had been a great War Minister and could have retired on his laurels. Or he might have revived the divided Liberal Party, or devoted himself to Land Reform, a subject to which he had frequently referred, and made a vast contribution to our agricultural development. Instead of which he formed a Coalition with the Conservatives which destroyed his personal influence and created a division in the Liberal ranks which has never been repaired. Moreover, his association with the Tories failed to enhance his reputation.

The Tories were themselves at variance. Lord Curzon had hoped to be Prime Minister; both Bonar Law and Austen Chamberlain distrusted Lloyd George. Lord Milner, who had been Secretary for War during hostilities, threatened resignation, but eventually accepted the Colonial Office. But prominent Conservatives accepted the proposed coalition because they believed Lloyd George would safeguard their interests. So Lloyd George embarked on a General Election, known as the

Khaki or Coupon Election, based on extravagant promises, greater production, national security, the creation of vast housing schemes, land reform and, in the language of Lloyd George, to create 'a land fit for heroes to live in'. Then the reality became apparent. The country was bankrupt. Speedy demobilisation which Lloyd George thought desirable despite protests released vast numbers of men from the Forces in conditions which were deplorable. Even Sir Edward Carson, not regarded as a social reformer, complained bitterly of the treatment meted out to ex-servicemen; the result was that instead of more employment the ranks of the existing unemployed were supplemented.

The General Election was a triumph for Lloyd George but a setback for Labour. Out of the 700 possible seats over 527 fell to Lloyd George and his slogans. Those elected had accepted the coupon which placed them in the hands of the Prime Minister. The Liberal Party was split from stem to stem, gaining only 33 seats. Labour did rather better by returning 59 members to the House of Commons. Herbert Asquith, who had been Prime Minister before being deposed by Lloyd George, was defeated. So was Arthur Henderson, the General Secretary of the Labour Party; and, regrettable as it was that this prominent politician should suffer defeat, I felt that it was even more regrettable that I, too, was defeated, in the first General Election in which I stood as a candidate.

My personal situation, however, was on the whole satisfactory. I was President of the Glasgow Trades Council, which had become more influential with the years, a member of the Glasgow Town Council and still a Parliamentary candidate for the constituency of Linlithgow. My opponent was James Kidd, a solicitor residing in the constituency, an exceptionally able man and a member of Lloyd George's Government. He was also supported by the Brewers' Association. Among the items in my election address was prohibition, which figured also in the election addresses of candidates sponsored by the Independent Labour Party in deference to the views of our leader, Keir Hardie, who began his political life in an Ayrshire constituency as a social reformer with emphasis on prohibition. The cause was featured in our programme again when I stood successfully for Parliament. This does not mean that large numbers of Labour Party members, or even of Labour MPs, were prohibitionists, but it is interesting to note that a prohibitionist called Scrymgeour actually defeated Winston Churchill in the 1922 election in Dundee. Obviously there was some encouragement at that time for the idea among the Scots.

Another item in my election address of some significance was Scottish Home Rule. It had some appeal for Scots, but this was more emotional than political. I was not advocating separation from the UK, but I was dissatisfied with the attitude towards Scotland of the Westminster establishment — frequent reference to the need for industrial development, but withholding the necessary finance from an impoverished country.

Although defeated, I had the satisfaction of receiving the highest Labour vote in any County constituency in Scotland. Best of all was that I made the acquaintance and eventually the sincere friendship of men and women in the constituency who had come into the Labour Party with an acceptance of its ideological principles and with the hope and high expectation of one day forming — or helping to form — a Labour Government, and creating a civilised society which would be capable of promoting well-being to every section of the community.

In the circumstances I had served my apprenticeship, and had succeeded in proving myself as an ardent, sincere member of the Labour Party without any hope of being more than a Member of Parliament, with a salary of no more than eight pounds weekly to maintain a home in Glasgow for my wife and two children and accommodation in London and, unlike the present situation, having to pay my fares between my constituency and home without any financial compensation from the Government. I had no knowledge of Marxian economics, of the theory of value or of Dialectical Materialism, but was solely and exclusively devoted to raising the standard of life of the working class, abolishing the slums, removing the squalor and filth and abominable conditions that prevailed in the industrial centres of Scotland, to say nothing of the hardships that existed in the Highlands of Scotland amongst the crofters and the agricultural workers.

Meanwhile, those who had listened and had read in the newspapers the high-faluting promises made by members of the newly formed Coalition Government, whether by the Prime Minister, Lloyd George, who was a Liberal, or the Deputy,

Bonar Law, who was a Conservative, were baffled by the pro-
crastinations and evasions and excuses which were ventilated in
place of improved conditions. Naturally there was resentment
in the industrial centres. The language used was harsh and
threatening. Unemployment was increasing; Social Security
was available but failed to provide a reasonable standard of
living. Those in the coalmining industry suffered incredible
hardships. Wages were low, hours were long, employment
insecure and, in the industrial centres generally, in shipbuilding, engineering and the like, nothing had been gained by our
glorious victory over Germany.

I was compensated for my earlier electoral defeat when, in
the General Election of 1922, I was elected MP for the constituency of the County of Linlithgow, otherwise known as West
Lothian, and joined several colleagues from the Clyde and other
parts of Scotland. The enthusiasm in St Enoch's Square in
Glasgow on the occasion of our departure for London was
amazing. Thousands of people saw us off, all optimistic about
the effect of our arrival at the House of Commons; and the vast
changes likely to occur as a result. All the slogans used during
the election with their assurances of beneficial legislation were
repeated — 'Away with unemployment'; 'Destroy the slums';
'No more starvation wages'; and 'What about Scotland?'

When I entered Parliament after the election of 1922, I was
not overawed by those around me. They were the products of
the high scholastic institutions — Eton, Harrow, Winchester —
and having seen and heard them I was consoled, at any rate for a
time, for my lack of education. Yet it must be made clear that
the lack of a sound education, the struggle to acquire knowledge, the need to be able to understand the meaning of every
paragraph one reads in a book or periodical, created an inhibi-
tion which I suffer even to this day. Two years of schooling in
London, nine months in South Shields, a year and a half in
Glasgow and leaving school before the age of twelve, and then
what? Reading, much of which I failed to understand, without
guidance or advice, maybe unconscious of ignorance; just forc-
ing one's way through the jungle, the hustle, bustle and rivalry
of political life, yet throughout it all seeking to retain the
characteristic to which I attach most importance, that of being
independent — all of these impediments could have been
avoided.

71

When the Coalition was abandoned in 1922 it had served both Lloyd George's purpose and that of the Tories. There was no evidence of agreement among the members of the Cabinet; Lloyd George's influence over politicians like Curzon or Bonar Law, even his erstwhile friend, Winston Churchill, a close colleague in the first Liberal Government, was diminished and practically negligible. In the election of 1922, although Labour failed to fulfil its expectation of gaining sufficient seats to form a government, we actually returned 154 candidates compared with 59 returned in 1918: seventeen of them came from Scotland and seven from Glasgow itself.

The fact that Glasgow had returned seven Labour candidates created the impression that our victories were influenced by the Russian Revolution of 1917. Glasgow was described as the 'Red Clyde'. As President of the Glasgow Trades Council, and member of the Scottish Trade Union Congress (not yet affiliated to the English section), I can assert that the Clyde was anything but revolutionary, unless a demand to deal with unemployment, rid ourselves of the slums and raise the standard of living could be regarded as revolutionary.

We lost no time on our arrival at Westminster; as member of the Independent Labour Party — the organisation which had sponsored my candidature and several others — I met my colleagues to consider the leadership of the Party. At a meeting held under the auspices of the ILP several names were mentioned, including J.R. Clynes, the existing Chairman, one of the textile leaders, and also Ramsay MacDonald, who was Secretary of the Party before the post was transferred to Arthur Henderson.

We argued about the subject but decided to leave it to a meeting of the Labour Party. At that meeting I proposed that Ramsay MacDonald should be appointed leader. This was opposed by some of my colleagues. Philip Snowden, as important in the eyes of members of the Party as Ramsay MacDonald, preferred that J.R. Clynes be re-elected. He was supported by most of my Scottish colleagues, Wheatley and Maxton among them. I pressed my point and demanded a vote. Ramsay MacDonald gained the victory over Clynes by five votes.

In the course of the debate on the King's Speech that took place after I entered Parliament, I listened to several speakers on the Conservative side which was then, of course, the Government side of the House, among them Nancy, Lady Astor, and Edmund Harmsworth. They, of course, as was natural, were defending Capitalism and resisting anything relating to Socialism. Nancy Astor was a remarkable person, lively and an excellent speaker though not well informed on political topics. She could be very waspish, and then veer round to remarkable generosity. Occasionally, when approached by some of my Labour colleagues on behalf of an institution in need of funds she would respond with her natural sincerity and generosity.

Nancy Astor was the first woman Member of Parliament. That is to say, the first woman who attended. Before her election a woman, Countess Markievicz, represented one of the Irish constituencies, but never took her seat. At that time quite a number of Irish Nationalists still remained in Parliament. I remember John Redmond, Tim Healy, Devlin and several others who belonged to the Irish Nationalists, and also the famous T.P. O'Connor, known as 'Tay Pay', at one time the Editor of the *Star*, a popular evening newspaper, who was Member for the Scotland Division of Liverpool, but usually represented Southern Irish opinion.

Among Nancy Astor's qualities was opposition to the consumption of alcoholic liquor. I have to admit that among some Labour Members, there was excessive drinking in the House of Commons and also at conferences. Among our MPs was a man named Jack Jones, the Member for Silvertown, a dockside area. He was inclined to absorb too much in the way of liquor, and often when entering the Chamber and a Member was speaking, would interrupt and make a nuisance of himself. Nancy Astor could not bear the sight of him, particularly when in his blustering mood, and one evening when Nancy was speaking he interrupted her. She replied with an admonition and a warning that if he continued to indulge in too much liquor it would have a deleterious effect on his stomach, to which he responded, 'I am ready to back my stomach against the Hon. Lady any time.'

The political ambitions of women members of the Party have been among the factors responsible for causing acute divisions in the ranks, many years before electoral suffrage was achieved in 1918. Yet, in my experience, setting aside the frenzy exhibited and the militant antics of some members of the Pankhurst

73

family, several women MPs, and others who failed to enter Parliament, were exceptionally successful. I recall Susan Lawrence, whose ability to deal with financial subjects in Parliament could compare favourably with that of any Chancellor of the Exchequer in my time, and Maggie Bondfield, the first woman member of a Labour Cabinet, whose humanity in matters concerning standards of living, housing, pensions and the like made her one of the great favourites in the Party; Marion Phillips and Ethel Snowden, the latter somewhat glamorous, one of the best women speakers in the Party. Nor can I forget Mary MacArthur, the attractive and able daughter of an Ayrshire draper who devoted herself to the protection of low-paid women workers. And, on the Conservative side, the late Baroness Tweedsmuir, whose ability would rank with that of the most able of Parliamentary Members. About those women of today engaged in political activities or social affairs and who have made reputations in or outside Parliament, I would prefer not to express an opinion; I have no desire to forfeit my somewhat fading popularity! Apart from the Suffragette Movement, the demand for what is regarded as female liberation began with the Women's Labour League, for which Margaret MacDonald, the wife of Ramsay MacDonald, was largely responsible. Unfortunately, she died in the autumn of 1911. It is a matter of conjecture to what extent the history of the Party would have undergone change, perhaps more beneficial, if she had lived. Undoubtedly she exerted considerable influence on her husband. MacDonald never re-married.

To return to the election. During the third day of the King's Speech I gained the ear of the Speaker and made my Maiden Speech. Frankly, I thought little of it. I was replying to arguments adduced by Nancy Astor and Edmund Harmsworth who were defending the Government's attitude on unemployment. The next morning, before returning to the House of Commons, I read *The Times* report of the previous day's proceedings and, to my surprise, they had singled me out as a person newly come to Parliament who had contributed to the debate like someone of long experience in the Assembly and, after referring to various speakers from the Labour benches who failed conspicuously to impress a Parliamentary audience, added:

Most of them were more sound and fury than solid debating material. Only Mr. Shinwell, the Linlithgow victor, made his mark as a political personality to be seriously considered.

The *Glasgow Citizen* and *Daily Express* wrote in glowing terms, and without any vanity or self-flattery I seek permission to quote. *Glasgow Citizen*, writing about E.D. Morel and Shinwell, said,

> Of the two Morel is the more impressive speaker, while Mr. Shinwell the more versatile. Each has a personality. Morel has the solider gifts of intellect and knowledge. Mr. Shinwell to mental gifts of a high order unites a remarkable quick-wittedness; he is specially conspicuous in extempore debate.

And the *Daily Express*:

> Following Lady Astor and Mr. Harmsworth he dealt point by point with them using all the mannerisms and conventions of Parliamentary debate as if he had been in the House for years instead of hours; displaying all the qualities that make a debater of weight and ingenuity. His utterance was slow and unhurried, and his method that of Socrates and Lord Carson. He made his mark by mastering the Parliamentary manner — perhaps his example will be taken to heart by the few remaining members who have not flashed their steel in debate.

Nevertheless, one must not make too much of high commendation from the newspapers, any more than to allow oneself to be depressed by their criticism. What is important for a Member of Parliament is that, whatever he says, he should receive some mention in the newspapers. To be ignored is to be humiliated; to be mentioned — even for harsh language which sounds unpleasant in the ears of one's colleagues — is important. However, I did note that none of my comrades from the Clyde tendered congratulations; I would have been more popular if I had made a poor speech.

Among those who accompanied me — or should I say that I accompanied — from Scotland to Westminster were some remarkable people. There was Jimmy Maxton, a wonderful orator, who could easily have become a Minister if he had cared. Jimmy was inclined to be a bit indolent; it was said that if he could help it he would never rise before mid-day. As for his oratory it was superb. There was John Wheatley, a businessman who became Minister of Housing in the first Labour Government and was leader of the Labour Party in the Glasgow Town Council for several years.

I write with some reserve about John Wheatley because when I was a member of the Glasgow Town Council he threatened to have me expelled from the Party because of my harsh criticism of the policy adopted by the Labour members. The Clyde MPs would have preferred him as a Party leader. There were others, like Campbell Stephen, a clergyman who had become a member of the Labour Party, amiable, scholarly, attractive, and David Kirkwood, principal foreman in the Munition Works in the East End of Glasgow during the whole of the war period, liked by almost everyone in the House of Commons despite political differences, and the harshness of some of his speeches delivered in an uncouth Scottish brogue.

Nevertheless, I express an opinion which is unfavourable; there was much disputation among the members of the ILP, to some extent consequent on the rivalries, jealousies that emerged because some were receiving no applause in the House, while others had become favourites with the leaders of the Party. Inevitably, some members of the ILP, all dedicated Socialists and undoubtedly sincere in their pressure for beneficial legislation, were at the same time almost enemies. This created the divisions in the Party. Some members were militants, others anything but Left Wing; in fact, some were far too much to the Right. As for myself, I was neither Left Wing nor on the Right, but exceedingly cautious about what I said. Sometimes, however, my speeches were somewhat harsh, even offensive, but never with the objective of becoming a Minister, and certainly not a leader in the Party, but solely to justify the confidence reposed in me by my constituents who had elected me to Parliament in the hope of benefits to come.

The Independent Labour Party was formed several years before the Labour Party, precisely in 1893, and was mainly the creation of Keir Hardie. It rejected the Marxist doctrine and had no revolutionary intentions. It sought to transform the Capitalist system into one capable of removing the harsh effects of poverty and unemployment. In particular it sought to remove class distinctions and use the Party machine for that express purpose. It is beyond question that the Independent Labour Party, in its consistent and effective propaganda, made a substantial contribution to Socialist thinking. It also was for many years responsible for sponsoring Parliamentary candidates and its first remarkable success was in the year 1922 when several members, including myself, entered Parliament. But in succeeding years the policy of the ILP gradually came into conflict with that of the Labour Party. It was more direct and positive in character and refused to accept the conventional view that by Parliamentary debate alone we could create a new form of society. This led to criticism of Party leadership and differences among several prominent members of the ILP, like Wheatley, Maxton and Buchanan, opponents of MacDonald. In the controversy I struggled hard to prevent the ILP leaving the Labour Party and, for some considerable time, was successful, but it was obvious that the differences became so acute when the ILP wanted not only to be responsible for propaganda, but to run candidates, that disaffiliation was inevitable.

We must not permit dissension of this or any other character to assume that the Labour Party will collapse. There have been many disagreements on policy even from 1900 when the Labour Representation Committee was formed. There are bound to be differences in a progressive Party. On the whole, although I find some activities of the so-called Left Wing militants distasteful, I recognise that substantial changes in the structure of the Party and in policy are inevitable. Speaking for myself, I don't require any help. I have been aware of the need for changes since I joined in 1903. The Left in the early days, the '20s and '30s, were mostly pacifists, against war or expenditure on armaments. Karl Marx was rarely mentioned. Now extremism takes the form either of dissension about leadership or slogans extracted from the *Communist Manifesto*, for which Marx and his colleague Engels bear the main responsibility, though seldom used in Parliamentary debates, but capable of creating the impression that Capitalism and all its works are in the process of exhaustion. One change is essential, and that is either to ignore, or even exclude, those whose primary concern is to gain the power of leadership. Leadership cannot be concentrated in one person. It is a matter for collective wisdom.

An MP like myself who gives hard knocks, indulges in harsh language, attacks his political opponents with immoderate severity, must be prepared for similar responses. Those including the Press media, who have disliked my political opinions, in particular my partisan advocacy of social policy, have used almost every offensive epithet in the dictionary in condemnation. This is what one must expect. Nor is it always inspired by malice or political hostility. Fundamentally, argument is the essence of democracy. However, there are compensations. I have already expressed my appreciation of the reception of my Maiden Speech in Parliament in 1922 and the unexpected applause from the Press. Many years later, in 1946, I had the honour of introducing legislation in the House of Commons for the purpose of transferring the privately owned mining industry to public ownership. I remember the euphoria manifested by members of the Labour Party, particularly those from mining constituencies; and their delight with the speech I delivered on that occasion. The general welcome and even the muted compliments from opponents — we had got the best of the argument — and even when enthusiasm faded because of the adverse climatic situation in which we found ourselves when the legislation was implemented; despite all the adversity and hostility, abuse and disappointment in certain quarters, the lack of sympathy from some colleagues, the hostility of the Press media, yet it was worthwhile to have achieved something in the political life of the country we had advocated for years.

8

In Ramsay MacDonald's Government

My pleasure at the favourable Press coverage soon evaporated. As I have said, there were no compliments from my colleagues. In politics you don't always achieve success by being too successful. If this observation appears to be contradictory it was a profound experience which was frequently emphasised during my membership of the House of Commons. Nevertheless, the Press coverage, however favourable, was insignificant. There were other problems to encounter and resolve, some of a financial character.

The salary of a Member of Parliament at that time was four hundred pounds annually, out of which one had to provide a reasonable sum for one's wife and children and sufficient for lodgings and food in London for at least five days in the week. In addition, MPs had to pay rail fares between their constituencies or homes and Westminster out of their own resources. Further expenses were incurred in replying to letters and, unlike the present situation, there was no franking of letters. This was an additional burden.

Before leaving for London several of my colleagues and I asked the headquarters of the ILP in London to seek accommodation, and George Hardie, a brother of Keir Hardie, and myself, were able to find lodgings in Pimlico, not far from Westminster. Two rooms were available, one priced at a guinea weekly, the other at fifteen shillings and breakfast could be provided for one and six each. Being younger than Hardie I suggested that I should occupy the smaller room at fifteen shillings, but would share the total cost of the two rooms with him. On those occasions when, owing to our inability to provide fares to return home, we had to remain in London at weekends, the situation worsened, and often we both had to seek food in the most dingy of restaurants. Often the charge for meat and two vegetables would be no more than a shilling. My experience was less serious than that of some colleagues who, we discovered, were actually suffering from lack of nutrition. Payment for MPs was unknown until the Liberal Government of 1911 when Asquith was Prime Minister. Under pressure from Labour Members and with the grudging acquiescence of Conservatives and Liberals he introduced legislation for payment of MPs. Before then the vast majority of Members relied upon their own financial resources. Some few members of the Labour Party received from their trade unions about two hundred pounds annually. There was certainly no financial incentive in seeking to become a Member of Parliament, however exalted the position was regarded.

This Parliament of 1922 was the most exciting — even turbulent — in my experience. It followed the upsurge of Labour support in the country and the return of several Members from the Clyde, from the North East and South Wales. It was also significant because of the obvious split in the Liberal Party, one section under the leadership of Asquith, the other, fewer in numbers, under Lloyd George. The main topic during the debates on the King's Speech related to the vast number unemployed and the threat of further unemployment. Ramsay MacDonald, the Leader of the Labour Party, pleaded with the Prime Minister, Bonar Law, that he should receive a deputation from the unemployed, to which the Prime Minister responded, 'This is a matter solely within the control of the Cabinet and we are not prepared to accept any dictation from any non-Parliamentary organisation.' It should be made clear that Bonar Law at this time was, to all intents and purposes, a non-leader and ineffective, for which his health was undoubtedly responsible. He only occupied the position of Leader of the Conservative Party and Prime Minister for the ensuing twelve months.

Among those who had been returned to Parliament for constituencies in the West of Scotland were several who had resigned appointments in business and the teaching profession. George Hardie was a consulting engineer, John Hay a teacher in one of the High Schools in Glasgow, McNeill Weir a journalist of distinction, John Wheatley a businessman unable to attend

(*Right*) My mother, in about 1911.

(*Below*) My mother, my sister Bessie, aged four, and myself, aged six. This photograph was taken in Leeds in 1890, at the wedding of my Uncle Harry who, a couple of years later, emigrated to South Africa with his father.

West Lothian, County of Linlithgow, in 1918: the first time I stood for election. I refused to support Lloyd George and was defeated. But I did gain a substantial vote—the highest Labour vote of the Scottish Counties. I am on the left.

(*Opposite above*) The Rockvale Football Club, 1900. I played centre-half, but as most of the team were rather older than me they appointed me temporary trainer. I am on the far right.

(*Opposite below*) My first wife, Fay, in 1902, at the age of twenty.

Plymouth Hoe. Playing bowls with some prominent trade union leaders while attending the 1925 Trade Union Conference. I was the Marine Workers Union delegate (second from the left).

(*Opposite above*) As Minister of Mines in the first Labour Government, 1924.

(*Opposite below*) At the 1928 by-election in West Lothian with Philip Snowden who spoke for me; I regained the seat lost at the previous election.

Keir Hardie (1858–1915) as Party Leader, 1906. He was the principal founder of the Independent Labour Party in 1894, and was instrumental in forming the Labour Party in 1900.

(*Opposite above*) The constituents who supported me in the 1935 election when I defeated Ramsay MacDonald.

(*Opposite below*) My youthful supporters—no votes but appreciated.

(*Left*) My style of speaking—persuasive, but I have to admit not always successful in persuading.

(*Below*) The Labour Cabinet in 1945. Front row (from left to right): Lord Addison, Lord Jowitt, Sir Stafford Cripps, Arthur Greenwood, Ernest Bevin, Clement Attlee, Herbert Morrison, Hugh Dalton, Lord Alexander, Chuter Ede, Ellen Wilkinson; back row: Aneurin Bevan, George Isaacs, Wedgwood Benn (senior), George Hall, Lord Pethwick-Lawrence, James Lawson, Joseph Westwood, myself, Ted Williams, Tom Williams.

to his commercial affairs because of his Parliamentary commitments. Indeed, almost everyone could have done better for himself than to become a Member of Parliament with a salary of four hundred pounds annually. Yet I cannot recall one single whisper of complaint about the pay, although they were far from satisfied with the conditions that existed in the House of Commons at that time.

In 1923 it was clear that another election was imminent. Stanley Baldwin was Prime Minister. There was considerable confusion and division in the ranks of the Conservatives. Dissensions on the subject of fiscal policy had weakened, but the rivalries remained. There were several candidates for leadership in the Conservative Party, but Stanley Baldwin was astute enough to realise that with internal dissensions, upsurge of the Labour Movement and the existence of a remnant of the Liberal Party, the time had arrived for another election. The result was sufficient to convince Baldwin that he might step aside, if only for a time, despite the Tories having the largest single Party membership with 258 seats, and permit some other person to deal with the growing problems created by our financial position after the First World War. So King George V sent for Ramsay MacDonald, the Leader of the Labour Party, which had gained 191 seats, to form a government.

The general opinion of Labour Members was that we should refuse office; the prospect of promoting beneficial legislation in the interests of the working classes with a majority of Conservatives and Liberals in opposition was unlikely, but MacDonald unexpectedly accepted office without consulting the Party Members and thus became Prime Minister. My personal view was that this was an error of judgement by MacDonald, and I doubted whether we could last more than a few months. MacDonald, in forming his Cabinet, selected several Conservatives and Liberals. Thus, in effect, the Cabinet consisted of a coalition. Obviously, this was unlikely to be acceptable to the new MPs, but that did not deter MacDonald. I had not the least expectation of becoming a Minister; but walking through one of the corridors when MacDonald, having already formed the Cabinet was considering who the Junior Ministers should be, I saw him with Pat Hastings who had been appointed Attorney General. MacDonald called me over and said, 'I want you to go to the Mines Department.' I was surprised at this invitation and suggested that as I knew very little about the industry it might be preferable to appoint one of the mining MPs, more knowledgeable on the subject and likely to be regarded with more favour by our colleagues. 'No,' said MacDonald, 'I want somebody impartial. You must take it.' I asked if I could have the opportunity to consider it in the course of the day, and consulted Philip Snowden, who strongly advised me to accept. So, after two years in Parliament, I became a Minister.

How did my family react to this event? As a child, I had no evidence of political interest or activity among members of my family. Few opportunities had been available for them, either in Holland or Poland, wherever they had lived (though it would seem that the situation in Holland was less repressive) to undertake political propaganda or express radical opinions. Even when I became a Member of Parliament members of the family seemed less than enthusiastic about my political associations. In discussion I failed to discover their political objectives, if indeed they had any, though I suspected they were pleased about the position I occupied. Socialism and anything associated with it they obviously disliked, and not until I became a Minister in the first Labour Government in 1924 was there any indication of — I hesitate to use the term enthusiasm — satisfaction that I had achieved some success. Obviously their attitude would be conditioned to some extent by Press criticism of the Party to which I belonged and about my activities. The only political support I can claim, so far as the family was concerned, was that my wife and my two elder children made it abundantly clear that my opinions and activities were, for them, wholly satisfactory.

Before long I realised that my appointment as a Minister was not regarded with favour by the general body of MPs, particularly those who had come from mining constituencies, but two of the Scottish MPs, both miners, Duncan Graham and James Welsh (the latter not only engaged in mining but also one of Scotland's poets), encouraged me to accept the position and assured me of their support.

However, there was little one could do in the Department. I recall my first day as Minister, arriving at the Mines Department in Millbank in pouring rain and meeting with some opposition from the doorkeeper, until I convinced him that I had been appointed Minister. Generally I received a most chilly reception from the officials. Indeed, the only person who appeared to be friendly disposed was the Permanent Under-Secretary of the day, Sir Ernest Gowers, one of the great Civil Servants. I became convinced, however, that William Brace, who was the Industrial Adviser to the Department and Labour Member for one of the Welsh constituencies, made no attempt to conceal his displeasure at my advent.

In the eleven months while I remained as Minister — the Government lasted no longer — I was able to introduce legislation for the provision of pit-head baths. This was a reform which I understood was demanded by the miners' unions. However, the legislation, although introduced, was not implemented until many years after. The majority in the Commons expressed no favour in support.

I met with some success when the miners threatened to strike and MacDonald, for some reason I failed to understand, instead of asking the Minister of Labour, Margaret Bondfield, the first woman Cabinet Minister, to undertake the necessary negotiations, instructed me to approach both miners and coalowners in the hope of preventing a dispute. I was successful in obtaining an increase of 13 per cent on the miners' basic wages. The coalowners, when negotiations terminated, maintained that I had held a pistol to their heads; thus it was announced in their Press. I had done nothing of the sort. The fact was that my success was due to an improvement in coal exports at the time, and the coalowners, though grudgingly, agreed to the increase.

There was one important subject in which I became intensely interested. That was the conversion of coal into oil products. A pilot scheme had been introduced by Lloyd George during the First World War at the Metropolitan Gas Works in London in the hope of meeting the energy needs of the Forces. But when the coalition ended so did the finance, and the scheme was abandoned. I discussed the matter with Philip Snowden with whom I had become friendly and who had become Chancellor of the Exchequer in the Government. Having also gained the support and encouragement of Dr Lander, the scientific expert in the Department, I obtained the sum of £30,000 to enable the scheme to be revived. Unfortunately, although a vast number of suggestions reached the Department from those who believed they had discovered the best process, we met with no success.

It is interesting to note that when we were back in opposition and Stanley Baldwin had returned as Prime Minister, I protested at the failure of the Government to provide the essential finance for the purpose of investigating the possibility of producing oil from coal and, in the course of my remarks, stated that so far as Scotland was concerned we had only touched the fringe of exploration. Of course, at the time I had no knowledge about the possibility of exploring oil in the North Sea, but I was aware that in some parts of Scotland, in my own constituency of West Lothian, we were producing oil from shale and refining it, although it was hardly a profitable process, and I had come to the conclusion that if we could produce oil from shale, with further development and the essential finance oil in greater quantity could be found in various parts of Scotland.

However, I encountered personal difficulties. I found it impossible to maintain a house in Glasgow and continue to pay for lodgings in London, and consequently decided to remove. With the assistance of a Member of Parliament, Charles Amann, a member of the London County Council, I was able to obtain a council house at Becontree, about twelve miles from Westminster. This was of some advantage, except that it increased my expenditure in payment of rail fares to and from Westminster.

During my period of office in those eleven months, apart from encouragement I had from friends in my constituency, I had the pleasure and privilege of meeting Lord Haldane, who had been a member of the Liberal Government before the First World War, and was appointed by MacDonald when he formed the Labour Cabinet. He had occupied the position of Lord Chancellor and also Secretary for War and in the latter appointment was responsible for the creation of auxiliary forces associated with the British Army. He occasionally invited me to his flat to meet himself and his sister. On one occasion he asked Lord Buckmaster — a famous political personality in the early part of the century — to enter into discussion with me on the subject of public ownership of the mining industry, and always maintained I had got the better of the argument.

Much has been written by various historians about Mac-Donald's reason for resigning as Prime Minister. There was the famous Campbell case, when subversive action against the Government was threatened by the insignificant Communist element in the country. Let me give the particulars. On 25 July, six months after the Labour Government had taken office, there appeared an open letter addressed to the Forces in the official organ of the Communist Party, the *Workers' Weekly*. The Forces were asked not to allow themselves to be used in industrial disputes. This issue was by no means original. The subject had frequently been raised during industrial disputes in South Wales, London, Glasgow and elsewhere. But it was part of a campaign by the Communist Party to prove that the Labour Party was the tool of reaction. Several questions were asked in Parliament which caused the Director of Public Prosecutions to advise the Attorney General, Sir Patrick Hastings, that action could be taken under an Act of Parliament of 1795, known as the Mutiny Act. Unfortunately, Sir Patrick, one of the most famous barristers of the period who had a great reputation in the Courts, was no politician and certainly not accustomed to Parliamentary procedure, and decided to take proceedings.

About a week later it appeared that the offices of the Communist paper had been raided and the Editor, J.R. Campbell, was arrested and charged with an offence. This led to an outburst from Labour MPs, not so much against Sir Patrick but against the Prime Minister; it was suspected that he was far from enthusiastic about the Russian Treaty which the Labour Government had previously entered into and was, in any case, glad to have an opportunity of denouncing the Communists. It was rumoured that he had instructed Sir Patrick to take action though, as it happened, this was a fabrication. I had personal knowledge that Sir Patrick was astonished and disturbed, because I happened to be sitting on the Front Government Bench beside him when he made it quite clear that he had no idea what all the fuss was about; he quite failed to appreciate the need for passions aroused by the event. It then appeared that the matter had come before the Cabinet and, although there was no evidence to substantiate the allegation of intervention by the Government, it was believed that an inappropriate action had been taken. The matter could have been disposed of quite easily if MacDonald had made a statement in the House clearing the Cabinet of any intervention; instead of which he announced with indignation that if either the Conservatives or Liberals decided to pursue the matter that would settle the issue so far as he was concerned, which, in effect, would mean his resignation.

A great deal has been said and written about the matter and even by professional historians who were apparently not aware that while the debate was proceeding in the House, initiated by the Liberal leader, Asquith, who was demanding an enquiry by Select Committee, MacDonald had gone to Downing Street, and I received a message asking me to go and see him. I had no idea what it was for. I went over and found him in the drawing room on the first floor, pacing up and down, obviously much disturbed. I asked what was the matter, only to discover that he was more furious about the criticism by some of his ILP colleagues, Maxton, Lansbury and others, than he was about the Liberal Party suggestion. I can recall saying to him, 'Pay no attention; all they are doing is repeating their election speeches. They have to in order to retain the support of their constituencies.' This, however, I admit had little effect. Then the telephone rang and Ben Scurr, the Chief Whip, came on the telephone and informed MacDonald that the Liberal Party had decided to press their amendment. 'That settles it,' said MacDonald, 'I shall have no more of it. I shall resign.'

His resignation preceded the election in 1924 when another incident occurred, the publication of a letter alleged to have been written by Zinoviev, the President of the Communist Third International, in which it was suggested that the British Communist Party should prepare for insurrection by the working-class areas of Great Britain, even to undermine the allegiance of the Forces. Whether there was actually such a letter or, indeed, if so, whether it was authentic, has never been settled. It was, however, enough to defeat the Labour Party. It may be asked why was it MacDonald sent for me? He was aware of my personal loyalty at that time; it could be also that I had frequently taken the Chair for him when he visited Glasgow, even during the war period, when he was engaged in his campaign 'Peace by negotiation'; not that I agreed with it, but it was customary for me, as Chairman of the Glasgow Trades Council, to take the Chair for most of the Labour and even Government celebrities who came to Glasgow. Moreover, I had proposed MacDonald in 1922 as Leader of the Labour Party when he succeeded in defeating J.R. Clynes, the previous Chairman, by five votes. As a result we had become friendly and occasionally I was asked to visit his unpretentious semi-detached house in Belsize Park in North London. On several occasions he confided in me about policy and about various members of the Party, even criticism of one of the most prominent colleagues, Philip Snowden. I should, however, mention that on one occasion Philip Snowden asked me to visit his villa in Golders Green, North London, where I had dinner with him and his wife, Ethel, and he, in the course of discussion, indulged in somewhat harsh criticism of MacDonald. I seem to have been a repository of both confidences.

Following the Lloyd George Coalition there were three General Elections, 1922, 1923, 1924. In the election of 1924 I found myself defeated in a straight fight. So were many of my colleagues, but in a by-election eighteen months later I returned to Parliament. During the period out of the House I was employed by the Seamen's organisation, undertaking part-time work and engaged in propaganda for the Independent Labour Party.

In the run-up to the election of 1929 the Labour Party had increased both its individual membership and affiliations from trade union organisations. The internal dissensions and incompetence of the Lloyd George Coalition, including the failure of Baldwin's protectionist policies, seemed to indicate that Labour at last was on the road to complete victory. I again contested the West Lothian Division, and won. After the poll was declared I decided to remain in my constituency for a few days, my intention being to visit various villages and townships and express my gratitude for being returned. However, I was forced to leave because of an express letter from Ramsay MacDonald. By this time it was discovered that we had failed to gain a complete victory, but it would be the largest single Party in the new House of Commons, and MacDonald would resume as leader of the Labour Party and Prime Minister. His letter insisted that I must return to London at once, and mentioned that he was having trouble about the formation of the Cabinet. Two days later I arrived in London and went to 10 Downing

Street. MacDonald then explained the purpose of his letter. The Trades Union Congress General Council had made demands on him about membership of the Cabinet. They had claimed that without their assistance he would not have been able to form a government. I asked, 'How does this concern me?' They had, so he informed me, expressed objection to my being in the Government because of a speech that I had made several weeks before the election at a conference in Birmingham, organised by the ILP, where I spoke about industrial democracy and in the course of my speech criticised the trade union leaders who had embarked on the General Strike of 1926. I had questioned whether it was wise to engage in a general strike without adequate preparation, considering the consequences either of defeat or victory. My speech was regarded as a vote of censure on the TUC. He must not have me in the Government.

Some time before the election I was engaged in conversation with Jimmy Thomas, who was for many years General Secretary of the Railwaymen's Union, again a Member of Parliament, and now appointed by MacDonald in his new Government as Colonial Secretary. In the course of our conversation he had prophesied that we would gain a complete victory at the election, and form a majority government for the first time. There would be a very important post for me, he said, probably at the Admiralty, which required reorganisation, and added, 'What we want is not only brawn but brains.' I paid little heed to this compliment — if, indeed, it was intended as such. So, when MacDonald told me about the protest by the TUC, I made it quite clear to him that he need not disturb himself: I would find myself quite happy on the back benches. 'Don't talk like that,' said MacDonald, 'just wait and see what happens. We have got to have you in somewhere.'

When I left Downing Street I went to a meeting of the ILP Administrative Council of which I was a member. They were in an office in Great George Street and were engaged in a discussion which ceased when I entered. Jimmy Maxton, influential and great orator, was in the Chair and asked, 'How did you get on with MacDonald?' They seemed to know what had happened. There was a general discussion in the course of which it was pointed out that although in the first Labour Government three members of the ILP were included — John Wheatley, a member of the Cabinet, Fred Jowett, also in the Cabinet, and myself as Secretary for Mines — there appeared to be no likelihood of an ILP member being included in the new Cabinet, not even Wheatley. During the discussion Pat Dollan, one of the most prominent Scottish members (not in Parliament, but better informed on Scottish Labour opinion than any other person), argued that it was important that somebody from the ILP should be in the Government, no matter what the appointment was. Maxton strongly opposed this; he preferred me on the back benches; but after a long discussion, without taking a vote, but after collecting the voices, it was decided that I should accept any position that MacDonald offered. I agreed most reluctantly.

Later in the day I telephoned Downing Street, spoke to MacDonald's Secretary — a man named Usher — and said I wanted to speak to the Prime Minister. During the conversation with MacDonald, I mentioned what had happened at the ILP meeting. He asked me to come round and see him the following day, which I did, and suggested that I should go to the War Office as Financial Secretary. I declined. I knew nothing about military affairs. I had been at the Mines Department and he agreed that I had done an excellent job there, taking into consideration the difficult circumstances of being in a minority, but he persisted and repeated, 'You have got to be in. In a few months the situation may change.' So I accepted, went to the War Office, and was ushered into the office of the Secretary of State, Tom Shaw, who immediately remarked, 'So you have come, have you?' It was clear from this that there had been considerable speculation as to whether or not I should be included. I said, 'Yes, I didn't want to come, but Mac asked me to accept and I will do whatever I am asked to do.' So my first experience of the War Office was in 1929.

I was there for almost eighteen months until MacDonald sent for me. When I arrived at Downing Street J.R. Clynes was with him. MacDonald said, 'You must go back to the Mines Department.' The reason was that the International Labour Organisation in Geneva were to consider a convention on hours of labour in the mining industry, and it was important that it should be endorsed. He did not think the existing Secretary for

Mines, Ben Turner, though a prominent member of the Party, would be able to face the task. He would not, in his opinion, be alert enough. I protested strongly about this and said, 'I did not want to accept the War Office job, you forced me to go. I would then have preferred the Mines Department, even though a junior post. Now you ask me to leave.' MacDonald persisted that I must accept it and, urged by Clynes, I did. The result was I spent six weeks in Geneva, most of the time attending the meetings of the League of Nations as observer, taking no part in the discussions — I had no right to do so — returning now and again to the International Labour Office, canvassing delegates in order to gain support for the convention which we considered necessary in the interests of British miners.

I was fortunate in obtaining the assistance and encouragement of Albert Thomas, who was Director General of the ILP. Despite opposition we were able to reach a favourable decision for a $7\frac{1}{2}$-hour day to be applied in every coal-producing country.

One of my supporters at the convention was the famous agitator Arthur Cook, General Secretary of the Miners, who, with forthright speeches, argued the miners' case, and also H.W. Lee, the Director General of the Coal Owners' Association of the United Kingdom, who argued against a $7\frac{1}{2}$-hour day because of additional cost to the mining industry. Cook was a Communist, Lee was Conservative, yet they were good friends. My intervention was regarded by MacDonald as most successful.

During this period the world was shocked by the exceptional financial recession that had occurred in the United States. Meanwhile, in the United Kingdom unemployment had reached nearly three million. The Government was attacked with harsh criticism at almost every sitting by the Conservatives, and also by the section of the Liberal Party led by Lloyd George, for its failure to solve the problem. The Prime Minister was forced to appoint a committee in the hope of finding a solution. The MPs appointed were George Lansbury, Commissioner of Works in the Government, Tom Johnson, Secretary of State for Scotland, Jimmy Thomas, Colonial Secretary, and Oswald Mosley, Member of Parliament but not holding any Government office.

During their deliberations Mosley formulated proposals with

which Thomas violently disagreed. I recall a special meeting of the Parliamentary Labour Party when Mosley endeavoured to obtain the support of the Party for his scheme. There was nothing revolutionary in his proposals apart from the need for substantial finance. The scheme was rejected by the Party, which led to the formation by Mosley of 'The New Party', later a Fascist organisation. A considerable number of MPs would have accepted the Mosley scheme, but were, like myself, suspicious about his intentions.

9

Out of Office — Out of Luck

The Labour Movement experienced several setbacks after the formative years at the beginning of the century, but when Ramsay MacDonald in 1931 decided to form a National Government in association with Baldwin, the Leader of the Conservative Party, and Herbert Samuel, the Leader of a section of the Liberal Party, it almost wrecked the Party. Only the hard core of the Labour Movement, consisting of some important trade unions and a dwindling, but faithful, number of individual members, averted complete disaster.

In the election of 1931 which followed Ramsay MacDonald's Coalition the number of Labour Members was reduced from 289, the number of seats gained in 1929, to only 46 with practically all the Front Benchers, consisting of Herbert Morrison, A.V. Alexander, Hugh Dalton, Arthur Greenwood and myself, defeated. Among Front Benchers only George Lansbury, Stafford Cripps and Clem Attlee remained.

For this setback — so disastrous in its effects — Ramsay MacDonald was undoubtedly responsible. Some professional historians and others who have written about MacDonald, including the events of 1931, hardly ever knew or met the man. With the exception of his son, Malcolm (who I admired greatly), none among the politicians was as intimate with Ramsay MacDonald as I was from 1914, although I had the privilege of meeting him in London before then in 1909, when I was a member of the Trade Board, appointed by Churchill.

In those formative years I admired him as our greatest orator. I occasionally visited MacDonald at his house in Belsize Park, London, and, apart from Alastair, his elder son, who was absent at that time, I met his other children, Malcolm, Ishbel and Sheila, and recall MacDonald asking me to visit what he

92

described as his study, just a tiny attic at the top of the house. During our conversation there was criticism of Maxton and a somewhat disparaging reference to Philip Snowden. When he went to live in Frognal he was unwell and talked about resignation. I persuaded him to abandon the idea. The historians can say or write what they like; I happen to understand more about the man, his purpose and character. Occasionally I would disagree with him, in particular when he somewhat petulantly complained about the sniping against him, often from some of his old ILP colleagues. On such occasions, and they were more frequent than I regarded as justified, I sought to explain their opposition. Nevertheless he found it disturbing, and damaging.

When, on occasion, MacDonald came to Glasgow to address meetings, I presided as an official of the Glasgow Trades Council which, in effect, was the Central Labour Party. When he began his campaign 'Peace by negotiation' during the war, although I was doubtful about it I agreed to take the Chair at a meeting, though aware his opponents threatened trouble. (I have already mentioned that it was the custom during the First World War, as long as I was President of the Glasgow Trades Council, to take the Chair for various celebrities associated with the Labour Movement, even though I disagreed with them.)

When the meeting at Charing Cross Halls in Glasgow was about to begin a report appeared in the newspapers that an organisation described as 'The Scottish Patriotic Federation' intended to disrupt the proceedings. When I arrived at the hall there was a crowd outside trying to force their way in. Two stewards held the door which had two glass panels, and with the utmost difficulty they resisted the efforts of some of the crowd to force their way in. I managed to get through because the stewards knew me, and went upstairs into the hall, where MacDonald, a woman speaker, Mrs Swanwick, and a fair number of people were present. When about to take the Chair I heard loud noises from below, so went to the head of the stairs to find out. I saw somebody with a very red face get his head in between the doors with the stewards struggling to keep him out. Without considering the consequences but determined that the meeting would not be disrupted, I ran down, saw this face and, with a quite ordinary punch with my right fist, got him between the eyes. Back into the crowd he went and doors were closed. I returned to the meeting where the audience waited to hear MacDonald's speech on 'Peace by negotiation'. MacDonald was not aware of what had happened until afterwards when I was accused of assaulting the man who intended to break up the meeting. The case came before the Stipendiary Magistrate who summed up the case, after hearing the evidence, by saying, 'Here is a situation where someone, or an organisation, according to Press reports, threatens to break up a meeting and then actually accuses the Chairman of the meeting of having assaulted him . . . I regard this as both fantastic and grotesque and dismiss the charge.' I expected MacDonald to be pleased: not at all; he disliked violence in any form.

During the period of office of the Labour Government in 1929 to 1931 there was vast unemployment, which had reached nearly three million by 1931, and all the forecasts were in the direction of substantial increase. It was decided to form a committee to investigate and to seek a solution. Those appointed were J.H. Thomas, Oswald Mosley, George Lansbury and, when the latter found it impossible to continue, Tom Johnson, Member for a Scottish Division who subsequently became Secretary for Scotland. Unfortunately, there was complete disagreement among them and, in consequence, Oswald Mosley prepared a memorandum in which he argued that for a period it might be necessary to postpone payments on the National Debt, which constituted one of the most severe burdens on our economy, increase expenditure on public works, stimulate consumption in order to provide employment, and the like. His most aggressive opponent was J.H. Thomas who was supported by Philip Snowden, then Chancellor of the Exchequer.

Here I must declare that of all my Parliamentary colleagues throughout many years, I know of none more warm-hearted and more ready to encourage younger members of the Party than Snowden. That he possessed, when in the mood, the most vitriolic tongue of any Member of Parliament I acknowledge, but his humanity and integrity were unquestionable. Unfortunately, however, he belonged to the Gladstonian period of free trade, balance of payments, and paying your way even if it meant reducing benefits associated with social welfare. The financial situation was so difficult that Snowden, as Chancellor of the Exchequer, decided to form a Committee, presided over by Sir George May, formerly Chairman of the Prudential Assurance Company, with the purpose of discovering how to escape from our precarious situation, much of which followed the American recession of 1929 which had disrupted international trade. The May Committee endorsed Snowden's policy, which led to dissension in the Cabinet. The Committee, among other proposals, made suggestions about the need for curtailing expenditure, including a reduction in Unemployment Benefit, and also legislation for protection against the import of foreign goods. Meanwhile, Lloyd George, the Leader of one section of the Liberal Party (the other was led by Herbert Asquith) constantly threatened the Government with defeat if it introduced Socialist legislation. Had MacDonald succeeded in 1929 in gaining a few more seats and forming a Majority Government, he could have ignored Lloyd George's threats and some proposals which emerged from the deliberations of the May Committee. Moreover, he could have brushed aside the demands of the Left Wing who, ignoring public opinion, demanded Socialist legislation of the most extreme character.

Those who believe that MacDonald acted in our interests without disrupting the Party of which he was Leader, are entitled to their opinion. I venture to disagree. There was in the House of Commons a room known as the Map Room, which was also a rendezvous for members of the Labour Party. On several occasions I recall MacDonald coming to the room, somewhat exhausted, admitting he was tired and worried but also suggesting, in view of our economic situation, the need for a Council of State. I have no hesitation in saying that my interpretation of those observations indicated that he regarded a Council of State — in plain words, a coalition — as a possible means of escape from national bankruptcy. Nor were his comments confined to the Map Room; they were heard elsewhere.

That MacDonald did not deliberately seek to destroy the Labour Party or prevent it from gaining power for many years I accept. But whatever his intentions there can be no doubt about how his mind was working. When after his decision I had the opportunity along with others to hear his explanation I protested as strongly as I could, and when he demanded from me what he should have done I replied, 'Remain as Leader of the Opposition.' 'Impossible,' he said, 'I must consider the interests of the country.' So for four subsequent years the country, industrially and socially, experienced, if not as harsh conditions as between 1929 and 1931, at least no better.

MacDonald's decision, disastrous for the Labour Party, was certainly a personal misfortune for me. He had asked me by telephone to remain in my post as Minister of Mines with the assurance that nobody would be allowed to interfere with my policy. My reply was, 'Despite my selection for the first Labour Government and also for the second, and our friendship, I must stand by the Party and therefore decline the invitation.' Two days later his Secretary telephoned me and said that Mac — as I called him — wanted to speak to me again. On this occasion he asked my views on who might be selected for the post that I decided to vacate. I was unable to offer any advice.

So I was out of a job. There seemed little opportunity of obtaining suitable employment. One of my best friends at that time was Jock Hyndley, later to become Lord Hyndley. I first met him in 1924 when Secretary for Mines. He was associated with several colliery undertakings, and had been appointed Honorary Industrial Adviser to the Mines Department. He was intensely interested in my activities, though he would often remark that I was splendid in the office but spoilt the good work by the speeches I made at the weekends. I have no doubt that when in financial difficulties after losing my seat in 1931 I could have borrowed money from him, but that would have disturbed our friendship. He advised me to see the London Director of the International Alloy Company of Canada who might offer me an appointment. I did so, found the gentleman most agreeable, and there seemed to be some prospect of employment on his staff, but before leaving his office he enquired whether I intended to remain in politics. I was unable then to give him a definite answer, but would consider it. However, when Arthur Henderson, the General Secretary of the Labour Party, heard from his son, now Lord Henderson, about my interview he sent for me and suggested that I could do both — accept the appointment if offered and also remain as a candidate in my constituency. I soon discovered that this was unacceptable: I could either accept the appointment and abandon a political career, or no appointment.

I had to refuse proposals which would have made life very comfortable for my family and self at an awkward time. The financial situation was precarious. Then Henderson saw me and suggested that I might undertake propaganda activities, financed by a fund set aside for the purpose. All he could offer was two hundred and fifty pounds annually; any expense in which I would be involved must be by the local constituencies, or myself.

Rarely if ever did any of my Parliamentary colleagues write to express regret about my defeat, and my reduced circumstances as propagandist for the Party. But how could I expect those who were defeated and in trouble themselves to be concerned? My two best friends in the Party at the time were Maurice Webb and Glenvil Hall who were officials at Transport House, one dealing with propaganda, the other in charge of finance, on whom I could rely for an advance on my salary to find sufficient funds for rail fares, other transport and accommodation when staying at some hotel. Incidentally, those subsidies were always deducted from my salary. Although the salary was far from enough I did not complain, but just made the best of it. (I had to mention it later.) Some people thought I received an enormous salary and they had to be corrected.

For the four years from 1931 until 1935, apart from a short leave during the holiday period, I would address anything from five to eight meetings every week. I must have addressed about a thousand meetings from Land's End to John o'Groats. I have to admit that those four years were the most miserable of my existence. Although I had experienced poverty as a child, even if unconscious of it, and in adolescence, and after I married endured the ills of poverty arising from unemployment, I never experienced anything comparable with the misery, depression, frustration and occasionally agonising feelings endured during those years.

As for my family, there was never any question of desertion or lack of affection. They understood my situation and, so far as my wife and two elder children were concerned, they did everything possible to ease my situation. Nowadays, when a Member of Parliament loses his Parliamentary seat through defeat or retirement his salary continues for no less than three months. There was nothing of the sort in 1931. Parliamentary ambition was a precarious affair, a gamble. Several colleagues were unable to return to their previous occupation; they had no other recourse than to seek Unemployment Benefit, and so were on the dole, like thousands of their constituents.

The custom in the kind of work I had undertaken was to accept hospitality, and here I must place on record the wonderful hospitality provided by members of the working class in the homes of miners, of shipyard workers and many others who were faithful to the objectives of the Labour Movement. On the other hand, I found hospitality from comfortable, even wealthy, members of the Party embarrassing: I was generally treated like one of the servants. Indeed, some of my experiences when accepting hospitality were of such a character that I eventually decided to stay at the cheapest possible hotels or boarding houses where the average charge was seven and six for bed and breakfast. Lunches I hardly ever bothered about. Breakfast in the morning and what was described as 'high tea' or dinner before going to a meeting sufficed, and even on those occasions when I stayed with people who provided hospitality I rarely went for lunch; I did without any.

Much of my time when not speaking was spent in those towns and cities with libraries, where I could read, or I did a great deal of walking. Miserable as life was I consider that my health in succeeding years, about which I certainly can't complain, was largely attributable to the long walks in which I indulged in various parts of the country during that period.

To write about all that I experienced would require several books. I content myself with a few anecdotes. On one occasion I was asked to undertake several meetings in South Wales. My itinerary was to start at Fishguard and then to visit all the important towns and end up at Newport. I had reasonably good meetings at Fishguard, and the comrades had arranged accommodation for me at the Fishguard Bay Hotel. My expectation was that the Secretary of the Constituency Party would enquire about my expenses, but there was no word from him and I was always too embarrassed to ask for them. The idea was that the various Constituency Parties would share my total expenses, i.e. the rail fare from one place to another and to and from London, including the cost of accommodation. At any rate, I failed to approach the Secretary at Fishguard, so I paid the bill. Usually before leaving London I would dip into my scanty resources for a few pounds or would ask the Finance Director at the Labour Party Head Office for an advance. However much I disliked this, it was often essential. The late Maurice Webb and Glenvil Hall, Finance Directors and wonderful comrades, understood my situation and helped.

From Fishguard I went to Neath with a similar experience, and also to Port Talbot, both with splendid meetings. Then on to Bridgend, then Barry Docks and to a suburb of Cardiff, and finally to Newport. By the time I arrived in Newport I had spent almost every penny I had. Not a single one of the officials had asked about my expenses. I stayed at the West Gate Hotel at Newport. In the morning I packed my bag; my intention was to catch an early train to London, but I had no money to pay the bill. I had hoped that because the Secretary at Newport was an old friend, I could at least speak to him in confidence about my expenses. Unfortunately, I learned he had gone to London on business. What was I to do? I had enough to send a telegram to my wife and ask her to sent me two pounds to pay my bill. Several times I went in and out of the hotel, wondering whether there would be a reply. Eventually, as there seemed to be no reply forthcoming, I decided I must take drastic measures and went off to look for a place where I could pawn my overcoat. However, not being very well acquainted with the town of Newport, I looked for the three brass balls in vain. Feeling very dispirited I decided to return to the hotel and seek compassion from the receptionist. On the way back, however, I saw a telegraph boy dawdling along; in those days they wore uniform. I wondered whether something was in store for me, so I followed him and, as it happened, he made his way into the hotel and I discovered there was a telegraph note for two pounds from my wife to enable me to pay the bill.

That was only one depressing experience among many I will never forget. Much as I deplore saying it, I incurred several bad debts there and in other places. The Head Office of the Labour Party always promised me that they would communicate with the local Secretary to obtain compensation; no doubt they did, but more often without any satisfaction.

I also had an experience in Scotland which embarrassed me. I went to one of the towns not far from Dundee. I have no wish to bring the blush of shame to the comrades there, so I will not mention the place. Anyway, it was long ago. After my meeting I was taken to a very slummy district to stay at the home of an old woman who I understood was occasionally asked to provide accommodation for speakers. I confess to more than disappointment with the bed, but even more with the breakfast placed before me in the morning. I was at a loss to know what to do with it. The last thing I wanted to do was to offend the old woman, so I indulged in duplicity. I told her that I always drank lots of tea before I took my breakfast: 'Could I have some more tea?' Whilst she was in the kitchen preparing the tea I took what appeared before me on the breakfast plate, put it in a piece of paper and into my pocket, and disposed of it when I left the building. The old lady told me she was paid two and six a night for bed and breakfast!

Another incident I recall was at Wakefield when I addressed a very large meeting and the Secretary asked me what my expenses were. I had addressed meetings in the area in various parts — Nottingham, Worksop and elsewhere — and I told him that my share of the expenses would be twenty-five shillings. He was astonished. He said, 'Only the other day we had Mr Wedgwood Benn here [the father of the present Tony Benn] and he only charged us a guinea.' I was aware that Wedgwood Benn, who had been a colleague of mine in the House of Commons, was a much wealthier man than I was, so I ceased to argue with the Secretary and said, 'I will accept the same,' which I did, and although on several occasions I received invitations to speak in the Wakefield area I never once did other than decline. The humiliation, the embarrassment that I suffered made those four years — forgive the emphasis and repetition — the most distressing, deplorable, objectionable period of my political life. I hesitate to speak about the number of places where I found myself, after the meeting, having to go to bed with the lodger. (To avoid any misunderstanding, let me say never of the female sex!)

Nevertheless, I had the knowledge that my speeches, which were well reported in the Press, particularly in the Provinces, had contributed to the upsurge of Labour enthusiasm in the following years. That helped partly to compensate for my distress. I was able to advise Transport House of what was happening throughout the country about our prospects; of the need for propaganda in certain towns and the lack of enthusiasm in many. Those activities in which I engaged during those four years, in supporting candidates in various constituencies, in obtaining some understanding of the character and ability of our candidates, was worth much more than the small fund available for propaganda in the possession of the Labour Party.

There is one event which furnished me with some pleasure. It occurred during my tour in North Wales. I was staying at a small hotel near Blaenau Ffestiniog. As my meeting was to take place in the evening I decided to go for a long walk. I must have walked six or seven miles, when I came to a tiny village which seemed to have only one street. I noticed there was a cobbler's shop there and, as my shoes were then in need of repair, I stopped and asked him if he would repair them for me. He was willing to do them and said I could call for them the next day. I explained that I had walked there and must return to my hotel, and he agreed to repair them while I waited. As he did so we talked and he told me that in the surrounding hills gold had been found in the past and although the hills were no longer worked for gold, Queen Alexandra's wedding ring had been made from the gold from that area. I took advantage of the information when I returned to my hotel by deciding to write a short piece in the hope of adding to my scanty financial resources. I sent it to the *Liverpool Daily Post*, who published it in their associated evening paper and I received, with gratification, a very useful sum of five pounds which helped to provide me with necessary sustenance for part of my tour.

When I returned from my tours, which usually lasted from eight to twelve days, I had to face the depressing presence of unpaid accounts. This meant a stint at the typewriter rushing off a few articles, mainly to the popular periodicals of the time like *Answers*, *Tit-Bits*, *John Bull* and also several for the *Daily Herald*. Usually the payment varied from five to ten pounds. In the case of *John Bull* when John Austin, a wonderful friend, was Editor, for a double-page article he would pay me what was regarded as the top price, fifteen pounds. I recall my relief on those occasions when sufficient articles were accepted by editors, and receiving in return, after a week or so, almost thirty pounds which enabled me to clear those hateful debts out of the way.

10

The Anxious Nineteen-thirties

However disagreeable it may seem to those who have expressed their admiration for my activities, my behaviour in those four years of misery had undergone an almost complete change. From my election in 1922 in the County of Linlithgow and my Maiden Speech, I had on the whole taken the view that if we were likely to achieve any of our objectives in the sphere of social reform, the removal of unemployment and the like, progress would be gradual and could not be attained merely by political bickering. Public consent was essential; the electors must believe in us and welcome our policy; and although during those years when I represented a Scottish constituency I criticised the Capitalist system and doubted whether our problems could be solved within the ambits of that system — if, indeed, it could be described as a system — my behaviour generally speaking would be regarded as moderate and agreeable. Unfortunately, those four years that I endured in my peregrinations throughout the country — the embarrassing hospitality, the dingy commercial hotels, the frustrating sense that I had adopted the wrong profession, the financial problems (a private fund in the possession of Headquarters from which they paid me less than five pounds a week which seemed like charity) and undertaking at least a thousand meetings with all the distaste involved — left me in no mood to be objective or even concerned about my behaviour. Therefore I make no complaint about Press criticisms of me occasionally; what they described as 'brawling' was not intended to offend but the result of a bitter experience. I was almost overcome by a sense of humiliation. There emerged a renewal of the bitterness that overwhelmed me when I was unemployed for several months after my first marriage, with no dole or Social Security benefits:

was this the social justice I had been advocating?

Unpleasant as my personal experiences were, they were in the circumstances inevitable. MacDonald's decision to join with Conservative and Liberal leaders in the formation of a National Government was of greater significance. Apart from the dislike which many members had for MacDonald, the Party was in process of actual disruption arising from disputes about policy.

The most active propaganda section of the Labour Party was the Independent Labour Party which, in 1932, had decided to disaffiliate from the main body. In substance this emerged from differences about future policy. A majority of ILP members were definitely pacifists and in opposition to expenditures on armaments. Another section declared that unless a future Labour Government, even though a minority in Parliament, decided on a comprehensive Socialist objective it was unworthy of support. To both criticisms and declarations I offered the strongest opposition.

Some of the frustrations suffered by the Labour Party between 1931 and 1935 were due to policy changes made by several prominent members. Oswald Mosley, already mentioned, who defected from the Conservative Party and had become a member of the Labour Party Executive, had formulated a political doctrine unacceptable to the Parliamentary Party, and created an organisation described on its initiation as 'The New Party', and gradually sought to emulate the activities and the Fascist philosophy advocated in Italy and Germany. Stafford Cripps, a brilliant advocate — it was said he made a fortune in the legal profession — had adopted an almost revolutionary attitude and proposed what was described as a 'United Front', making advances to the ILP, the Communist Party and the extreme Left Wing of the Labour Party. In this effort he sought to involve myself and Alfred Barnes, who was regarded as one of the leaders of the Co-operative Party. Following a conversation Barnes and I had with Cripps the latter produced a formula, and we both asked for time to consider it, to which Cripps agreed. However, we discovered the following day that it had been prematurely disclosed to the Press by Cripps, without consultation.

The core of the Labour Party, reduced in numbers in 1931,

was practically helpless, largely, as I have already said, because of its lack of experienced personnel. However influential a member of the Labour Party as an MP may consider himself, outside the House of Commons he is of little consequence. That was the situation in which the small body of Labour MPs found themselves. Moreover, so far as the Coalition leaders were concerned, the period between 1931 and 1935 was one of duplicity and deception: they achieved discontent at home and distrust abroad.

Baldwin, the Leader of the Conservative section of the Government, had managed to demote MacDonald who became President of the Council, and as Prime Minister sought to force another election, the principal purpose to be support of the League of Nations, collective security and, consequently, reduced expenditure on armaments. Subsequently, months after the 1935 election during which he had gained the victory, he confessed he had postulated collective security and appeasement because — to his own language — 'What success could I have achieved if I had said we must arm ourselves in preparation for war against Germany?'

Meanwhile I continued my propaganda for the Labour Party. One of my difficulties, speaking almost every night and sometimes three or four meetings at the weekend, was to find subjects to talk about, particularly when I found that meetings were attended by interested people who went to more than one meeting in some industrial districts. I was often also instructed by Headquarters to speak in constituencies where a new candidate was addressing his or her inaugural meeting. Some candidates I found worthy of support; others were almost illiterate, some were casual. In one constituency where I arrived at a rather large meeting, and had to speak before the candidate had arrived, I found the audience expressing much appreciation of my remarks. When the selected candidate arrived his opening remark was, 'I had the greatest trouble getting here and now I am here I don't know what the hell to talk about.' The interest I had created speedily evaporated.

In another constituency on the coast of Northumberland I found a number of the audiences were in-shore fishermen, making a living, and not much at that, with their small fishing boats. To my astonishment the candidate sought to arouse interest in the audience by suggesting nationalisation of the fishing industry, which naturally was the reverse of what they expected, and I had the task of correcting that blunder.

Frequently, I would find myself speaking alone with a candidate, even one actually selected to fight a constituency, who would address a very ordinary working-class audience on the subject of Foreign Affairs, and both in language and policy which I myself had difficulty in understanding.

I must confess it was a relief when, in 1935, after four years, I found myself selected as a candidate for the second time. On several occasions, even in the '20s and '30s, I had addressed meetings in the North East, in the counties of Northumberland and Durham. The Member for Morpeth in Northumberland was Ebby Edwards, one of the most prominent and friendly miners' leaders, who intended to retire in 1935. I met him when addressing meetings in the area, and was one of the principal speakers at the Annual Gala of the Northumberland Labour Movement when he mentioned that I should be a candidate for Morpeth on his retirement. At the same time it was suggested that I might be nominated, along with others, as a candidate for the Seaham constituency where Ramsay MacDonald was Member of Parliament. So, without any definite decision, I could anticipate the possibility of becoming the candidate either for Morpeth or Seaham. As it happened the Selection Conference in Seaham came before the meeting at Morpeth. At Seaham there were over twenty nominations. Some of the local people who were nominated were well disposed and decided to withdraw. However, after addressing the members of the Executive at Seaham, I found myself selected to contest the constituency at the next election against Ramsay MacDonald. I must confess that despite my success it was not entirely agreeable. After all I had proposed MacDonald as Leader of the Party in 1922 when he was opposed by most of my colleagues of the ILP, including Philip Snowden, James Maxton, John Wheatley and others. I had also refused the invitation to join his Government in 1931. Now I was selected as the most likely person to defeat him. I was popular, yet far from happy.

However, I fought the election. Most predictions in the Press were that I would fail to defeat an ex-Prime Minister and Leader of the Party; that I would fight the election in an arrogant fashion and, according to Jimmy Thomas, Mac-Donald's principal trade union supporter, would indulge in bitter invective of a personal character. There was apparently no doubt that I would be defeated. Despite all the rumours and forecasts I never mentioned MacDonald's name during the whole of the contest, nor indulged in any personel vilification or abuse. Although I succeeded in obtaining a majority — much to the surprise of the Press and even Labour Headquarters — of nearly 21,000, whatever my personal sentiments were, I just regarded it as my duty and responsibility, as a loyal member of the Labour Party without any notion of revengeful opposition to MacDonald, to defeat him.

I had to contend, on my return as MP in 1935, with the disturbing impression that although I had defeated Ramsay MacDonald and had gained the plaudits of the crowd, I was anything but secure. Among those who were delighted that MacDonald was defeated — the Party seemed to be revenged for what happened in 1931 — there were several who were certain that they could have won the seat if selected as candidate, though this seemed to be an afterthought. So, from my return as Member of Parliament for the Seaham constituency, which later became Easington, there was always a queue lined up in the expectation that either age or some other factor would pave the way for another candidate.

I dare go even further. Friends in the constituency time and again on my frequent visits — almost every week at conferences, public meetings, functions and the like — would whisper in my ear, 'Some of them are after your seat.' And prominent persons connected with the constituency emphasised that as the miners' MPs were under an obligation to retire at the age of sixty-five that should also apply in my case. The late Sir William Lawther, one of the most prominent miners' leaders in the North East, stated on a platform at a Durham Miners' Gala where I was one of the principal speakers that one day Seaham must become a seat in the possession of the miners, to which I was bound to respond, and with some vigour, when called upon to speak, that I would remain a Member for the Seaham constituency as long as the people wanted me. I remained a Member for thirty-five years, but under no illusion about the ambitions of quite a number of people in the constituency who were not beyond suggesting that I might be run over by a bus! To come down to brass tacks, I was told by a Councillor, a member of the Easington District Council, that he had seen the General Secretary of the Durham Miners' Union, Sam Watson, who told him that 'he did not expect that Shinwell would last much longer and therefore that he should prepare himself to become a candidate for the seat'. Now, let it be clearly understood that though I had gained the victory, and with the plaudits, enthusiasm and the hullabaloo, and with thirty-five years of membership, it was anything but a safe seat. I came to the conclusion that the smaller the margin in victory the safer one is. But who wants a marginal constituency when ambition urges the search for the safe seats?

The repeated efforts of Neville Chamberlain to reach agreement with Hitler in order to avoid conflict, though appreciated by some Members of the House of Commons and even a few in the Labour Party, were nullified by events. Churchill's frequent warnings in the months preceding 1939 were more realistic. My own experience when visiting Germany as far back as 1930 when Secretary of Mines contributed to my belief that Churchill was right and the advocates of appeasement were wrong. Following the creation of the Weimar Republic I made several visits to Berlin to engage in negotiations with Dr Schumacher, who was associated with the German Trades Department. Our purpose was to eliminate unnecessary competition which was adversely affecting the coal industry both in Germany and the United Kingdom. Even at that time, probably due to rising unemployment and inevitable discontent, I saw trucks crowded with men shouting apparently abusive slogans directed against the Weimar Government. The impression I gained at the time was that these demonstrations were associated with the Communist element in Germany, and inspired by the Soviet Union. Such militant demonstrations influenced the Right Wing elements in Germany to indulge in similar demonstrations from which, eventually, Hitler took full advantage. Gradually it became obvious to those Members in the Commons who were concerned about the international situation that conflict was imminent. I recall the memorable occasion when Neville Chamberlain, after one of his frequent visits to Germany and consultations with Hitler, was received in the House of Commons with dwindling enthusiasm and was forced to remark, 'I have some friends here.' Ultimately the realities of the situation could not be concealed, and despite apprehensions about lack of preparation to engage in conflict, for which the Labour Party was as much, if not even more, to blame than the Baldwin/Chamberlain régime, there was always excessive optimism about the prospect of peace. Churchill was the outstanding exception.

The Annual Labour Party Conference was held at Bournemouth in May 1940, when the news of conflict was conveyed by Clem Attlee, the Party Leader, to a joint meeting of the Labour Party. Several trade union leaders who were members of the Council of Labour were present and also members of the Parliamentary Committee of the Labour Party, which some years later became known as the Shadow Cabinet. As a member of the Parliamentary Committee of the Party I was in attendance.

The possible successors to Neville Chamberlain were Lord Halifax and Churchill. There was no possible contender in the ranks of Labour. Leopold Amery might have been a candidate: he was one of the ablest members of the Conservative Party, for whom apart from political views I had much admiration. Both Amery and Arthur Greenwood, a prominent Front Bench member of the Labour Party, almost simultaneously on receipt of news about an imminent attack by Germany on Poland, spoke in patriotic terms, regardless in the circumstances of our lack of preparation. Aggression against Poland would not be tolerated and was unacceptable to all but an insignificant minority of pacifists in Parliament. We, in our wisdom, decided to support Churchill.

Churchill was in process of forming a new Government, though still First Lord of the Admiralty, when the Labour Party Conference was about to debate the report on Parliamentary proceedings in the current year. This was the responsibility of the Party Leader. It was customary for the Party Leader to report on Parliamentary activities at every Annual Conference. It was suddenly announced that Churchill had asked for Attlee to go to London, apparently for the purpose of discussing the situation, although it was clear to members of the Conference when this became known that something more than a discussion was likely. As Attlee had to leave for London he asked me, as a Member of the Parliamentary Committee, to take his place and deal with the Parliamentary Report. Meanwhile, Arthur Greenwood accompanied Attlee to London.

In the course of replying to questions concerning items in the Parliamentary Report, a message came to inform me that Winston Churchill was on the telephone and wished to speak to me. I asked the messenger to inform Mr Churchill or whoever had given the message that I was engaged on the platform at Bournemouth, but would telephone Mr Churchill at the conclusion of our proceedings which was expected after five o'clock. I then telephoned and asked for Mr Churchill's Secretary, and then Churchill himself spoke to me. 'I want you to take full charge of Food in the House of Commons,' were his actual words. I thanked him for the invitation, but declined, saying it was not a subject in which I was expert, but assured him that if we were engaged in conflict with Germany I was as anxious as himself to ensure that we would help with our utmost capabilities; 'but I would prefer not to accept the position.' He said, 'I am sorry about this. I understand your colleagues [by whom I presume he meant Attlee and Greenwood, who were meeting him in London] want you in.' I responded, 'They have never mentioned it to me.' He expressed his regret and, indeed, on many occasions thereafter when I happened to meet him he would say, 'I always wanted you in.'

The next morning I learned from the Press that Bob Boothby had accepted the post which I had refused. I am convinced that if he had known that I had refused the invitation he would not have accepted a post which would hardly justify his capabilities. As one of the ablest politicians, far abler than several appointed, he would have expected something higher in rank. Even then he only served about a year when a dispute with Churchill caused his resignation. What it was about I have no idea.

I recall our return to London when we met in the Commons on the Sunday after the conclusion of our Conference. To meet on a Sunday was exceptional. While we were in the Chamber we heard the siren and assumed we were about to be bombed. We were ushered down into the lower part of the House and after a few moments learned that this was no act of aggression but one of our own aircraft in action.

One of the most significant incidents immediately after the

conclusion of the Conference and before we left Bournemouth was the antics of some of my colleagues. The telephones in the Highcliffe Hotel were fully occupied. All sorts of rumours were current about appointments to the new Government. The most impressive incident was the hysterical activities of Hugh Dalton, who seemed to want all the telephones for himself. He fully expected that he would be asked to join the War Cabinet, and believed that such a position was well within his capabilities, no matter what view was held by his colleagues. His expectations were doomed to disappointment, for, several days afterwards, amidst controversy, rumour and much excitement, it was announced that Dalton would become the Minister of Economic Warfare, an appointment far below the standard he had set for himself.

My refusal to join Churchill's Government was the subject of some criticism from colleagues, even from my constituency, and I learned later that Attlee was furious. When we returned to the House of Commons, Arthur Jenkins, his Private Secretary, father of Roy Jenkins, came and told me that Attlee wished to see me. I found him less angry than I understood he was likely to be. 'Why did you not come and tell me what Churchill had offered? I might have been able to wangle something different.' I replied, 'I didn't want you to wangle anything for me; I did not expect an appointment. In any event, I was not going to accept an appointment for which I had no obvious competency. I shall do very well outside the Government.' That ended our conversation.

I claim no credit for refusing Churchill's invitation. On the contrary, I appreciated his invitation, and it may well be that if I had accepted the appointment and had full charge in the House of Commons, since the Minister, Lord Woolton, would be in the House of Lords, it might have been to my advantage, but I have no feeling of regret or disappointment, and certainly no bitterness about the matter. However, it was not the first time I had refused an invitation from a Prime Minister, as MacDonald knew when he formed his National Government in 1931 and asked me to remain at the Mines Department. I repeat, there were no regrets.

11

The External Enemy

My exclusion from Churchill's Government of 1940 — my personal decision as I have said, though I was grateful to the Prime Minister for his invitation — was nevertheless a disappointment. I should have liked to make my contribution and, if offered a post associated with shipping, a subject, as mentioned in a previous chapter, on which I was reasonably well-informed, no doubt I would have accepted. But to accept a post — even though in charge, as Churchill suggested in the House of Commons, with Lord Woolton as senior Minister in the Lords was not agreeable.

It was believed in some quarters that my refusal was due to dislike of coalition. It was not. In peace coalition would make no appeal to me; in a situation where our nation is at war, unity in the political sphere, as in all essential activities, is a responsibility which every one of us must accept. Of course I might have suggested another post, but call it what you please; obstinacy, vanity or even stupidity? I have never asked for a post in any government, whether in Ramsay MacDonald's first or second government: I was a member of both. I did not seek inclusion in 1931, and though invited I refused to join Mac-Donald's Coalition. Nor did I approach Attlee when he formed the government of 1945 in which however I was included. So when I took my rightful place on the Opposition Front Bench in 1939 as an elected member of the Parliamentary Committee, which later became known as the Shadow Cabinet, I felt no resentment. All I wished to do was to express my opinions and make my contribution to victory. Though I was frequently critical, even using strong language and asking what were considered by some of my Labour colleagues in the Government awkward questions, I never opposed the Government on any matter which would impede their efforts towards success. On the contrary, I advocated the creation of a department associated with production, a proposition which at first the Government rejected, and a few months afterwards accepted and appointed Oliver Lyttelton, who later became Lord Chandos, as Minister. It is interesting that when he was appointed he sent for me and for at least an hour we discussed policy and what should be done in order to justify the existence of the new Department.

In almost every debate I was closely associated with our design for victory; shipping in particular, about which I became even better informed during the war because of my association with various shipping firms. I was frequently in possession of information — regrettably, of our losses at sea — which was not available to Members of the House of Commons. I was also involved with prominent Members on both sides of the House, irrespective of Party, in demanding a vigorous prosecution of the war effort; efficient organisation; the removal of all restrictions on production and, in particular (although as things developed this might well have been premature if accepted), a Second Front.

My activities during the war were of so varied a character that my postbag some weeks reached about five hundred, mainly from members in the Forces. So active did I become that I was forced to employ two secretaries during most of the war period. I wrote innumerable articles for the public Press and for magazines; even for some foreign periodicals and, as an indication of my thoughts and purpose during the war period, I venture to produce an extract from my article in the *Fortnightly Review* entitled 'Design for Victory'. I would not wish to weary those who may read this book with the whole article.

> We can rest assured, if Hitler is able to establish a line in Russia that he can hold with a portion of his present attacking forces, he will use the coming winter in feverish and stupendous preparation for the annihilation of this country. Practically the whole of continental Europe is his workshop, and its population his slaves.
>
> These considerations are advanced in no spirit of fear for the future. On the contrary, I am of opinion that with the proper organization and employment of our vast resources, plus the invaluable and greatly-increasing aid of the United States, we can win.

There have been dislocations, misdirection and palpable confusion to which Parliamentary critics, in the national interest, have drawn attention.

In the main the critics have been completely justified, although they have not always been understood. Ministerial irritation, however slight, cannot cancel out healthy and constructive advice. If it were to do so, then the whole concept of Parliament as a free debating assembly and executive of the nation would cease to have any meaning.

In 1943 I was approached by Brendan Bracken, the man most intimate with Churchill at the time, who asked whether I would be prepared to consider accepting the position of Minister of Fuel and Power. I understood that Gwilym Lloyd George was the Minister, and asked was he going to retire. 'No,' said Bracken, 'but he may be transferred to the Ministry of Food. What we want you to understand' — and I presume that by 'we' he meant that Churchill was involved — 'is that there can be no question of nationalisation.' To which I responded, 'During the war everything, more or less, is nationalised and at present I have no political views on the subject. But if I am asked to accept, one thing is essential; that is, in order to get the coal we want we must make an exception as far as rations are concerned for those in the mining community. They must be increased.' Bracken agreed.

When, in the course of that day, this proposal became known to Clem Attlee, he sent for me and without asking me any questions expressed himself in angry terms about such an appointment. He had not been consulted. Without losing my temper — Attlee's attitude did not alarm me — I said I had not asked for the appointment, I had merely been asked if I was prepared to accept it, and assumed that he must have known about it. Even that did not satisfy him and he remarked that because I had refused to join earlier there were others more entitled to it than I was. That ended the dialogue. Whether Attlee had intervened or not I don't know. Eventually the information was conveyed to me by Brendan Bracken that Gwilym Lloyd George had decided not to leave his Department, which had no depressing effect on me. I had not asked for the job, did not necessarily want the job, and was quite content to associate myself with the Government in a vigorous prosecution of the war. And on that remarkable occasion when a number of my colleagues, led by Aneurin Bevan, put down a Motion of 'No Confidence in the Government' I remarked that I wanted not one Motion but two; one 'No Confidence in the Government' and another a 'Motion of Confidence in the Prime Minister'. When the vote was taken the number in favour of confidence in the Government and the Prime Minister numbered over four hundred as against the insignificant minority of twenty-five. I voted with the majority. My suggestion was considered to be out of order; some thought it frivolous.

I confess that in order to make many speeches on several subjects connected with the prosecution of the war, and later on post-war reconstruction, although there was access to information in the libraries of the House, I had recourse to the Labour Party Information Department and to those who were experts on various subjects. For example, I required special information on a financial subject and approached the Labour Party, who were unable to satisfy me, but suggested that I might make contact with Dr Thomas Balogh (now Lord Balogh). I did so and became quite friendly with him, and am bound to admit he was of considerable value in preparing memoranda and providing me with information on subjects about which I was far from competent. My differences with him were that although he was regarded, no doubt deservedly, as a prominent economist and an expert on Foreign Exchanges, he was not versed in political methods; in my opinion, no politician. I admit at once that I am no economist, but with information in my possession I have the capacity to present it, which is the function of the politician.

As for shipping problems, I was aware of our dreadful losses at sea and the failure frequently of our convoy system. My information was obtainable from Lloyd's Register and from several shipowners, who not only furnished me with information but two of whom offered me an appointment as political adviser. Incidentally, I had other offers financially agreeable, but have always regarded myself, ever since I entered the political arena, as a full-time politician. I don't deny undertaking some writing and broadcasting for financial gain, but never have been associated with any business concern. I had the advantage of friendship with several important newspaper editors who used my services, which I agree was profitable to me, if not altogether satisfactory to the readers of those periodicals. Indeed, unlike many of my colleagues who have been critical of the Press and Pressmen, though I have been the victim of harsh criticism and abuse from that quarter occasionally, I strongly hold the view and have said so repeatedly, that a politician or, if you like, a Parliamentarian, always ready to speak his mind, irrespective of the consequences, must not be unduly disturbed if he is knocked about in return, even by the Press.

Almost at the outset of hostilities a significant number of Parliamentarians in the three political Parties favoured further efforts in the direction of appeasement. Lloyd George was convinced that further negotiations with Hitler would be fruitful; he declared that without the aid of Russia we did not possess the military capabilities to defeat Germany. There are some on the Labour side whose pacifism was in evidence; among them were Nye Bevan and Sydney Silverman, both effective Parliamentarians who, though not against hopes of victory, formed a group to embarrass members of the Government on a variety of subjects. My own position was unequivocal. When our country is at peace it is inevitable that those opposed to the Government should criticise and submit an alternative policy, but when the nation is at war and the fate of our people is at stake, it is the responsibility of every Member of Parliament, irrespective of ideological views and objectives, to render the responsible government the utmost encouragement. On the occasion afore-mentioned when I sought to effect a compromise and suggested that we might have two votes of confidence, one of confidence in Mr Churchill as Prime Minister, the other of no confidence in members of the Government, and my proposition was rejected, it created no hostility or bitterness between some members of the Government and myself. Maybe there was some amusement.

I found myself frequently at loggerheads with Ernest Bevin, who was Minister of Labour, and while appreciating his industry and patriotism I indulged in criticism of his dictatorial attitude which I venture to describe as suitable for a trade union leader, but repugnant to those of us who were familiar with the democratic process of a Parliamentary institution. Undoubtedly a great Minister of Labour: I am not so sure about his achievements when Foreign Secretary.

Now, a few comments about Prime Ministers, just to establish my claim to have known every Prime Minister from the beginning of this century, with two exceptions; the Marquis of Salisbury, the Prime Minister in the Conservative Government when I first entered the political arena in 1903, and Sir Henry Campbell Bannerman, who was Prime Minister until superseded by Herbert Asquith in 1908. I had heard Bonar Law, a Canadian businessman who had been encouraged by Sir Max Aitken (later Lord Beaverbrook) to enter politics and had become the Member for the Gorbals Division of Glasgow in 1900. Reference to his candidature in 1906, opposed by George Barnes, the Engineers' Secretary, when my frequent interruptions led to my ejection from the meeting, has already been made. Balfour, the intellectual; Asquith, so dignified; Lloyd George, great War Minister; Stanley Baldwin, Conservative, I found, although politically hostile, friendly and approachable. Ramsay MacDonald, admired for his oratory; Anthony Eden, a competent Foreign Secretary who had the courage to resign when member of the Chamberlain Government; Harold Macmillan, ablest of Tory Prime Ministers, who, when he first entered Parliament, sat on what would then be described as the Cross Benches and made speeches of a Fabian character, adopting as his policy what was described as the Middle Way.

And in the following years Clem Attlee, Alec Douglas-Home, Ted Heath, Harold Wilson and Jim Callaghan. I have known and have heard them all speak; on the whole, politics apart, men with patriotic instincts and more or less effective leadership. For more detail see, if you care, my book *I've Lived Through It All* (1973). Among them all, the one I found almost intolerable was Neville Chamberlain. No doubt a person of strong character with a high reputation because of his interests in Local Authority affairs, but his manner seemed so dictatorial, his contempt for opponents so obvious; yet he undoubtedly assumed that he had always adopted the right course in seeking to avoid conflict through appeasement.

Frequently, when asked to advance some reason for my admiration of Churchill, which has frequently evoked astonishment, I have referred to those memorable speeches he delivered in the House of Commons and repeated on the public platform, containing warnings about the possibility of conflict and the need for preparation. I confess that this admiration was in sharp contrast to my sentiments about Churchill in the early '20s and to some extent even in the period before the First World War when he was a member of the Liberal Government. It was my privilege to be invited to contribute to a series of articles in a book entitled *Churchill by his Contemporaries*, edited by Charles Eade, one of the most prominent members of the newspaper world. The request made to me was that I should contribute an article as from 'a political opponent', in which having agreed I referred to Churchill as the most able and bitter of our opponents in the '20s and '30s, when he described the Labour Party as 'unfit to govern'. About industrial development and standards of living for the working class — indeed, on most aspects of social policy — he encouraged no admiration from members of the Labour Party, but during those few years before 1940 in my opinion he spoke as a prophet; in the event he was proved to be right.

Those memorable speeches made before the Second World War were ignored by Baldwin and Neville Chamberlain, who had both been responsible for Cabinet appointments of people who were pygmies compared with Churchill. How often did I observe the ostracism, the snubs, the waspish remarks, and deplore Churchill brooding through the corridors accompanied by one or two friends, when it would appear that he was, for the rest of his political life, to remain in the wilderness. I recall his determination in June of 1940:

> We shall not flag or fail, we shall fight in France, we shall fight on the seas and oceans, we shall fight with growing confidence and growing strength in the air, we shall defend our island, whatever the cost may be, we shall fight on the beaches, we shall fight on the landing grounds, we shall fight in the fields and in the streets, we shall fight in the hills; we shall never surrender.

And the contrast in 1945 after his dismissal from office:

> On the night of the 10th May 1940, at the outset of this mighty battle, I acquired the chief power in the State, which henceforth I wielded in ever growing measure for 5 years and 3 months of world war, at the end of which time, all our enemies having surrendered

117

unconditionally or being about to do so, I was immediately dismissed by the British electorate from all further conduct of their affairs.

When Churchill was returned in 1951 I stated the policy of the Labour Party on the international question as follows:

> We of the Labour Party accept the need for defence preparations because at present there appears to be no satisfactory alternative. But, simultaneously, we must direct attention to the need for promoting peace in the diplomatic sphere.

In this debate Churchill said, following my speech,

> . . . the spirit which has animated the Rt. Hon. Gentleman in the main discharge of his great duties was one which has, in peace as well as in war, added to the strength and security of our country.

And in the same debate:

> . . . I should not like the speech of the late Minister of Defence to go without its due and proper acknowledgement from this side of the House. We have our party battles and bitterness, and the great balance of the nation is maintained to some extent by our quarrels, but I have always felt and testified, even in moments of party strife, to the Rt. Hon. Gentleman's sterling patriotism and to the fact that his heart is in the right place where the life and strength of our country were concerned . . .

We have in our time paid one another compliments and hurled our invective. When the Churchillian periods were honeyed I have on occasion suspected the political motive behind them. But I accepted the fact that in the security of a new Parliament Churchill as Prime Minister was extending his hand across the barrier of party. How high this man could rise above the midget stature of his colleagues! It was not unamusing to watch their faces as Churchill intervened in this way. *Hansard*'s pages record no approval from the benches behind him for his remarks.

12

A Second Chamber — Pros and Cons

Although I was fully occupied during the war period with speeches in Parliament, Questions, and association with various organisations, I found time to indulge in writing a vast number of articles which task I found very profitable, so much so that I was able to purchase a modest house in Hampstead Garden suburb in North London. It had a lovely garden with gorgeous beds of roses, a perfect delight. The cost of purchase was almost derisory compared to existing prices of similar dwellings. When sadly my wife died I decided to leave and dispose of the place. If retained it would have proved a most valuable asset; but I regard financial losses of that character as of minor consequence compared to the loss of a wonderful partner whom I married at the age of nineteen and lived with for fifty-one years.

I was invited later to write a book for the publishing firm of MacDonald. It appeared in 1943 under the title *The Britain I Want*, more appropriate to peace than war. The contents presented in broad outline the line of policy which might be adopted by a post-war government; a general raising of living standards, improved educational facilities, modern transport, and though not actually advocating public ownership of key industries and services, the inevitability of change. Beyond doubt in my view the sacrifices of war called for a more contented and beneficial peace. Much of what appeared was closely related to policies advocated by a Committee on Post-War-Reconstruction formed by the Labour Party in 1944 of which I was appointed Chairman; some of the proposals were implemented by the Attlee Government of 1945.

A politician, to be effective, whether in the course of his Parliamentary duties or other responsibilities, must have the

119

capacity to adapt himself to changing situations; even firm ideological convictions require to be reviewed in the light of changing circumstances. At the outset of my political career my speeches and activities were not based on any particular ideology, but rather due to my environment, the social iniquities, personal hardships and the belief that social justice, which was interpreted as ending unemployment, the surrounding squalor and the frustrations of poverty, could not be regarded as associated with fixed ideas about society. One was simply the victim of one's environment, and thought and acted accordingly. Naturally, in the course of time one either created a philosophy for oneself or relied upon the wisdom and knowledge of others. I therefore confess that my views and activities associated with those views have been modified, and though hardly to my credit I admit this has a bearing on my acceptance of the invitation to become a member of the House of Lords. I venture to include some extracts from *The Britain I Want* which explain my attitude:

> In a true Democracy, that is a state of Society where there is economic as well as political equality, there can be no place for class distinctions. Ancestry and accumulated wealth do not, of themselves, establish the claim to true nobility . . .
>
> Let us be frank about all this title business, and admit that it is archaic and wholly unnecessary. It adds nothing to the stature of any man or woman, who by his or her public-spiritedness or accomplishments has earned general approval . . .
>
> Greatness of character, courage, supreme achievement in the fields of science, literature, art, music, government, have their own reward in the happiness they bring to those who properly appreciate them. Would the handle of a knighthood or a baronetcy have added one degree to the immortality of Shakespeare, or Robert Burns, or Abraham Lincoln? Would *Macbeth* be a greater drama, or the *Cotter's Saturday Night* be more sublime, or negro liberation a more profound reality? Assuredly not. The dignity of public life is not increased by the periodical addition to the Peerage. But the system of class distinction is perpetuated, as it is by other means.

The question may well be asked, 'Why, in view of the observations just quoted, many honours conferred have been found acceptable, including membership of the House of Lords?'

There are two possible answers. One is the well-known adage, 'Other times, other manners.' For other honours conferred upon me I have never asked or expected.

My acceptance of the invitation to join the House of Lords was not an ideological change; my political opinions are perhaps modified but unchanged; it was just a geographical transfer. And it should be noted that it has some historical justification, as the following lines will demonstrate:

> King David and King Solomon
> Led merry, merry lives.
> They had many, many ladies
> And many, many wives.
> But when old age crept over them
> They had many, many qualms
> So King David wrote the Proverbs
> And King Solomon wrote the Psalms.

If they could change their activities why should it be regarded as improper for me?

There are other reasons why, in spite of my opposition to class distinctions, I accepted an invitation to become a member of that august assembly. Far too often people are elevated to the House of Lords without regard to accomplishments which have earned general approval. Even if some of these recipients are entitled to an honour, there are many thousands of people scattered throughout the community who receive no official recognition. Supreme achievement in the fields of science, literature, art or government should provide their own reward in the contentment they bring to those who have made their contribution. Then what is my justification? When I reached, in 1970, the age of eighty-five, without any expression of opinion by the principal members of the Labour Party in my constituency, I informed them of my intention not to stand for re-election, but with the assurance that my physical and mental faculties were still of some value I accepted the invitation in the hope of making some contribution.

Now that I am a member of what is generally regarded as the nobility — I won't dare to say aristocracy — the demand made by the Labour Party for abolition of the Upper House is in a personal sense irrelevant. It is unlikely to happen in my time.

Nevertheless, I express an opinion. Despite all the arguments adduced, many vehement in character, and disparaging methods deployed by the House of Lords in legislation, I reject the concept of a single chamber. Legislation of whatever character must be thoroughly digested by an impartial body, whether elected or nominated; the final decision must rest with the House of Commons. I am equally opposed to the creation of an elected Second Chamber. To be elected involves authority, but a body of people with expert knowledge and, as far as possible, unbiased, with authority to examine and suggest amendments to legislation that emerges from the House of Commons, is commendable. I want, however, in the light of the economic and industrial situation in the UK and the general world situation with which we are fundamentally concerned, not to spend too much time on a constitutional matter of this sort.

Recently it was stated that in the House of Lords there are thirteen members who are Fellows of the Royal Society; most of them professors or lecturers in science, and among them are prominent industrialists. Moreover, we have in our midst a vast number of famous economists. Indeed, so far as the House of Lords is concerned, there is no assembly in the world like it. Nevertheless, despite their deliberations they remain puzzled and baffled by events. There is a high standard of debate but seldom implementation. Ability, yes; solutions, none. I do not believe that all wisdom resides in the House of Commons, nor is it confined to the House of Lords; but a combination of both, concerned with the national interest, would seem to me a reasonable and feasible proposition.

There is a simple and possible solution to the opposing views that can be immediately implemented to remove much of the discontent; namely, reduce the number of hereditary peers in the Upper House to abolish the imbalance and anomalous superiority of the Conservatives over the Labour or other Opposition. This is a modest demand that would be acceptable, in my judgement, not only by members of the Labour Party but also by many Conservatives. Naturally, being non-elected it could not expect to be vested with authority, and should remain essentially advisory in character. The term revising, so frequently used, is irrelevant. It is illogical to seek authority to revise legislation in the knowledge that the elected House of Commons can always ignore the proposed revision. We have to consider in future in any reform of our Parliamentary institutions whether to accept consensus or embark on confrontation. In the circumstances, for the preservation of our democracy, and so far as it is practicable, I prefer consensus.

Opposition to the House of Lords remains a subject of acute controversy in Labour Party circles. As a result of anti-trade union legislation in the early part of the century and the reactionary attitude of hereditary peers, the demand for the abolition of the House of Lords became one of the main demands of the Labour Party, although hotly rejected by successive Governments. Even in Conservative ranks there are many who agree that there exists an imbalance in the membership of the Lords and that a reduction in the number of hereditary Peers would be desirable and more acceptable. Within the ranks of Labour the demand is clear and forthright for abolition, though far from unanimous. Only about two years ago a Labour Party Conference carried a resolution on the subject; six million votes against ninety thousand. Several eloquent speeches were made, one by the mover of the resolution, Jack Jones, then the General Secretary of the Transport and General Workers' Union, in the course of which he said, 'I cannot really believe that modern men and women want to keep an unnecessary and very costly institution in being. It really is a luxury which we have tolerated too long and a luxury which we should proceed to end as quickly as possible. I say that the toleration has gone on too long. It represents a danger.' And he added, 'We cannot reconcile the House of Lords with the basic thinking of trade unionism and the Labour Movement for which we stand.' And he further added, 'I tell you that the House of Lords is a symbol of paralysis and reaction and there is no dignity in that. Three-quarters of the members of the House of Lords inherited their position by birth; their ancestors were, by and large, cattle robbers, land thieves, and a few were Court prostitutes.'

I was present at the Conference as an *ex-officio* member where the above arguments were used and ventured to offer a few observations. I reminded the Conference that one of Labour's principal objectives was to prevent unemployment. Yet they were proposing in their resolution 'to dis-employ one thousand people at a stroke'. I also mentioned that 'sooner or later the House of Lords must be either reformed or abolished, but reform of the House of Lords would be as difficult as reforming the European Economic Community'. There would be constitutional difficulties but, in any event, Labour must first of all win the next General Election. I also reminded the Conference that it was customary in Labour circles, when people were removed from their employment, to provide them with what is called 'redundancy payments', and added, 'Let us be practical about it. The overwhelming majority in the House of Lords, even among the aristocratic members — and not all are on one side of the House — even some members of the Labour Party are also agreed about reducing the number of hereditary Peers. Perhaps this is the method some members of the Labour Party would prefer.' I note in a report of the proceedings, 'There was prolonged applause . . .' If my arguments failed my speech was found agreeable.

Since then, the first essential to which I directed attention, namely winning the General Election, has met with failure, so for the moment the Lords can sleep peacefully in their beds. Meanwhile much can be done to redress the imbalance in numbers that quite improperly still exists in the Lords. There are several institutions in the United Kingdom which are outmoded; maybe the House of Lords is one of them. It may not please everybody, but in a democratic and fair-minded country like ours it is unable to do much harm.

My transfer to the Lords induced *Vogue* magazine to enquire about my normal day which I include in this story:

MY DAY

My day invariably spills over from the night before. Between eleven thirty and midnight it is time to retire; the prospect of reading free from distractions is attractive. Several books are available by my bedside. I read for perhaps an hour, am drowsy, drop off to sleep, involuntarily, hardly aware of it, waken around three a.m., the light full on, books on the floor, my spectacles missing; find them under the bed — my day begins.

Now for the mystery, why do I always waken at three a.m.? No rational explanation, nor hope of further slumber for at least two hours. Return to reading. My favourite books; Shakespeare indispensable, *The Hundred Best Essays* by Earl Birkenhead, Bertrand Russell's *History of Western Philosophy*, *Churchill by his Contemporaries*, and his *Great Contemporaries*, biographies and autobiographies, histories galore; to dip spasmodically; I find past events of absorbing interest. So settle down and select the book by Russell, an intellectual encyclopaedia, a fascinating study of distinguished metaphysicians, among them Descartes, Hume, Spencer, Kant, Schopenhauer, Spinoza and Bergson; I must discover the inner meaning of the latter's dissertations on the twin subjects of time and space, which don't appear to make sense and offend my reason. I am in good company, Russell agrees, I prefer to rely on his wisdom. Put book aside, tired of reading, lines and words mingling, sight blurred, try to sleep, no use, so reflect on world problems; anxiety about South East Asia, Korea may go next, maybe Malaysia; turbulence in Middle East, situation depressing. Turn to cosmic problems, meaning of the Universe, future of mankind, what is purpose of life, why am I here? A veritable jungle of thoughts; rational and consecutive thinking difficult in the small hours before dawn. Drowsy again, try to sleep, fail, pick up Parliamentary report of House of Commons debates. MPs bickering, Party squabbles, exciting dialogue on inflation, economic and industrial affairs; subject of excessive taxation is mentioned, nobody appears to have any solution; a junior member representing the Treasury intervenes, to the accompaniment of cheers and jeers. All quite unlike the House of Lords where debate is dignified, though somewhat soporific.

Now am able to sleep, wake at six a.m., spasmodic thoughts, six-thirty, better get up and make tea; take cup to wife; this gesture strongly recommend to all husbands, nothing contributes more to domestic harmony. Newspapers arrive, read leading articles. Same theme with variations; one paper suggests Harold Wilson should resign, another is convinced that Prime Minister is firmly resolved to tackle the militants and deserves the full support of his political opponents. Mrs. Thatcher reported to have made brilliant speech, worthy of a potential Prime Minister; Ted Heath makes a comeback; and so on. Postman rings, delivers mail, many papers, some official, bills, can almost smell them, fan mail following radio programme in which I call for more patriotism, one letter, anonymous, writer considers time I retired, two letters from schoolboys, one asks me to get him a German military helmet, the other asks for definition of politics to be published in school newspaper, send two quotations from Mrs. Gandhi and Mr. Heath; a request from university undergraduate for interview, seeking information on political event when Ramsay MacDonald was Prime Minister. To these may be added statement from bank, depressing, and a couple of suggestions from charitable organisations to send donations. Put aside for consideration. Decide to have some breakfast, consists of grapefruit, cereal, two slices of wholemeal bread, marmalade and small slice of cheese; however, feel must cut down, putting on weight, so far a balanced diet. Examine diary for engagements. Promised to lunch with business friend at first-class restaurant, House of Lords two-thirty, function at seven-thirty for eight (not every day, but too often).

Spend rest of morning at typewriter, dispose of correspondence, so far as practicable. Must not miss lunch engagement, keeps down household expenses. Business friend talks his head off, has ready solution for our problems; Government no good, workers won't work, too greedy, want the earth. Listen with respect, get word in edgewise, ask what is alternative to existing Government; body of businessmen essential. I modestly suggest that businessmen when occasionally associated with governments have not proved entirely successful. Lunch proceeds on muted tones, even the smoked salmon fails to raise temperature, two double whiskys more help-ful. Lunch over, I invite business friend to lunch with me some time, no date fixed.

Hail taxi, ask driver to take me to House of Commons. 'Sorry, sir,' he says, 'thought you were now in the House of Lords.' I reply, not for the first time to inquisitive taxi drivers, 'As an ex-member of the Commons am entitled to use Commons' entrance.' Eventually arrive at Lords, have question on Order Paper, ask it, get unsatisfactory answer, ask few supplementaries, replies even more unsatisfactory. Listen to some speeches, feel sleepy after bad night, repair to library, find all comfortable chairs occupied, some writing, some reading, would you believe it, a few aristocratic peers, and a few recently ennobled actually slumbering? House up about six thirty, an early night, can go home.

Decide to stay in library for a while, read magazines, feel sleepy so leave. Depart through House of Commons, meet MPs, all irrespective of Party, express felicitations, hope I am well. Characteristic of British political life, all friendly. Possible to be on excellent terms with members of Opposition despite violently differing opinions. Leave to get taxi. Bell rings at New Palace Yard gate for taxis. We queue up, first come first served. Occasionally an MP with own car offers a lift.

Arrive home after frustration through traffic jam, greet wife, customary salutations, ask if any phone calls, none, something wrong, am being neglected, must do something about it. Dinner ready; usual reference to rising cost of fish or meat, enough to spoil appetite. Decide to have aperitif, complete harmony established. No work tonight, ask what's on TV, any Westerns, answer, no, but excellent symphony orchestra after news, says I must listen. Help to wash dishes, have a smoke, recline on settee, sleepy, wake up half an hour later, have another smoke, get ready for bed, same routine, same kind of night, same kind of reading, with, of course, variations, same amount of sleep. What a day, hope for more exciting day tomorrow.

13

Minister of Fuel and Power

To return to the narrative of events, after the digressions in the last chapter.

In the final weeks of the year 1944 and the early part of 1945, despite the advent of a new German missile, described in slang terms as the 'doodlebug', capable of causing much devastation, a revised climate of opinion emerged. Despondency was replaced by optimism and assurance of victory which could now be achieved through the co-ordinated efforts of the Allies, though somewhat belated. Had both the United States and the Soviet Union entered the affray some months earlier hostilities would have ended and thousands of lives been saved. Neither Roosevelt, nor any of his American colleagues, were displaying anxiety about the salvation of Europe or preventing disintegration of the British Empire; the Soviet Union was concerned primarily about its principal enemy, Germany.

Now that victory was in sight the sentiments of the British public were transferred to prospects of post-war reconstruction on a vast scale producing beneficial changes in social and industrial policy, and of a General Election capable of injecting reality into our superficial democracy. On few vital issues was there complete unity among the political parties. Winston Churchill, admired as the saviour of his country, was convinced he could win an election based on his reputation, yet preferred a continuance of the wartime Coalition, until a Japanese surrender was achieved, and expressed vigorous opposition to the possibility of an early election.

Following negotiations between Clem Attlee and his Deputy, Arthur Greenwood, with Churchill now in the role of Prime Minister of a shaky Coalition, the Labour Party Conference met at Blackpool and in the evening of the opening session of that

128

Conference there was a joint meeting of Labour's National Executive and the Parliamentary Committee of the Labour Party. I was there as a member of both, and our purpose was to hear a report from Attlee who, by his speech, created the impression of agreement with Churchill. Members who were present were almost equally divided. Ernest Bevin, who had occupied a prominent post during the war period as Minister of Labour, could claim to speak for the Trade Union Movement and agreed with Attlee. So did Hugh Dalton; even Herbert Morrison expressed doubts about a Labour victory if an election occurred at an early date. Other Members favoured the opposite view, Nye Bevan and myself among them. I had expressed my personal opinion for many weeks before, based on a vast correspondence received from members of the Forces, indicating expectation about social progress and expressing desire for changes. The correspondence was endorsed by huge demonstrations where, with enthusiasm, members of the public applauded militant speeches. At our meeting no vote was taken, but Attlee, in his usual fashion, collected the voices and concluded that a majority rejected a continuance of Coalition and preferred to contest an early election as an Independent Party. It was decided that Churchill should be notified accordingly. On the following day at the opening of the Conference, when the decision was announced, there were thunders of applause, which must have surprised Attlee and others who had advocated a continuance of the wartime Coalition. The Conference decision was consistent with my expectations.

The election of 1945, despite Press opinions and forecasts, gave Labour a majority of 184 and returned to Westminster a substantial body of new Members of Parliament intoxicated with their success. In their enthusiasm they sang 'The Red Flag', and yelled 'Carry out Conference decisions', 'Get on with the job', 'Teach the Tories a lesson', and 'We are the masters now.' Nevertheless, behind the euphoria conditions were more realistic. To begin with there was disquiet in the Cabinet. Stafford Cripps, whose sanctimonious manner and high moral pleadings sometimes distorted loyalty to colleagues, wanted somebody other than Attlee as Leader. So did Herbert Morrison who coveted the post for himself, based on his services to the Party. Cripps actually telephoned Morrison, suggesting that the election should be delayed to enable MPs to elect a new Leader. Morrison made it known that he was reluctant to serve as Deputy under Attlee, while Hugh Dalton, disappointed in his expectation of, at the very least, being head of the Foreign Office, blamed Attlee, and some time later referred to the Party Leader in one of his famous whispers, which could be heard the length of a Commons corridor, as 'That bloody little man.' Such preliminaries were among the sentiments which later provoked the conspiracy to replace Attlee with Ernie Bevin, to Bevin's credit the suggestion was treated with contempt.

Following the war a financial crisis was inevitable. Britain was unable to pay for essential imports. Rationing became unavoidable. It even reached the stage when bread was rationed. A policy of austerity was fashioned by the Treasury and endorsed by Dalton, whose ambivalence was exposed, more by faith than fact, by the 'song in his heart' and 'good prospects are around the corner'. Attlee endured with calm the effort to replace him by some other Leader. Previously, during the war, there had been several conspiracies against him during his leadership; one organised by Ellen Wilkinson, the other in which Arthur Greenwood was involved, though the latter resented the conspiracy to replace Attlee by himself.

In the formation of his Cabinet Attlee paid appropriate regard to the services of those colleagues who had been associated with him and Churchill in the wartime Coalition. To my surprise he sent for me and said, 'I want you to go to the Ministry of Fuel and Power. You will be in the Cabinet and will be responsible for the nationalisation of the mines.' He also appointed Aneurin Bevan as Minister of Health, who reasonably might have expressed surprise. We were both, during the period of war, indulging from time to time in criticism of Attlee and Government policy. As regards myself, I was not suspect of any opposition to vigorous prosecution of the war, just proposing what I considered were constructive proposals which could actively assist in ensuring victory; nor was there any reason to assume that Nye Bevan's activities were subversive, except that he often indulged in criticism, using language which would seem to convey his personal dislike for some members of the Government.

Thus, having been appointed to take charge of the Ministry

of Fuel and Power, I went to Millbank and, after some discussion with an inquisitive doorkeeper, was ushered into a room to meet the Permanent Under-Secretary, Sir Donald Ferguson.

At a subsequent meeting when several officials of the Department attended I informed them of instructions I received from Clem Attlee, and enquired whether any documents were available on reorganisation of the coalmining industry in the event of public ownership. The reply, considering the nature of the request, was in the negative. There had been, some years before, an enquiry by the Sankey Commission, but the subject of nationalisation was not regarded as relevant to that enquiry. There was a report by Sir Charles Reid, the Ministry's eminent mining engineer, into reorganisation based exclusively on continuation of private ownership; nothing more. Thereupon I enquired whether any documents or blue prints were available at Labour Party Headquarters. None was available apart from resolutions advocating public ownership carried at frequent conferences, and a few pamphlets, for which Arthur Greenwood was responsible, presented in general terms. Thereupon I was informed by the Permanent Under-Secretary that it would fall to me to furnish the main principles to be embodied in a Parliamentary Bill.

The absence of blueprints, basic principles or administrative details either in the Government Department or in the Labour Party and the lack of a Working Party to prepare them is a defect which must be avoided preceding further nationalisation. It is interesting to recall that when addressing a meeting in 1947 of the Co-operative Union at Edinburgh I pleaded for more effective study of the problems associated with public ownership. To my surprise I was rebuked in a letter from Jim Callaghan, who went so far as to suggest that by my declaration I had rendered a disservice to the Party. Of course this was not long after my esteemed colleague had entered Parliament, so I did not complain.

There was another occasion at a meeting of the Parliamentary Labour Party when I warned members to be cautious before proceeding with schemes of public ownership and to consider all possible consequences. I was dedicated completely to the principle of nationalisation, but experience has convinced me that vast changes in the administration and control of industry

131

must be carefully thought out. I was astonished when Richard Marsh — now Sir Richard — who had not long entered Parliament, made an eloquent and bitter attack on me for using such language. Since then, however, Sir Richard has been Chairman of British Rail and must have discovered the validity of my observations.

I was aware that the Cabinet majority view— a few, including myself, favoured Parliamentary control — was based on Herbert Morrison's intervention many years before in dealing with London Transport, to proceed on the basis of a public Corporation taking over the industry, including all its assets, but free from Parliamentary intervention, involving effective accountability and the expectation of being able to pay its way; and on this basis we proceeded to prepare legislation. I then decided on what was, in my judgement, the proper course, namely, to enter into consultation with the representatives of the miners and of the mineowners. From the latter I received, as I expected, the somewhat negative suggestion that I should leave well alone, despite their knowledge that the industry was almost insolvent, and incapable of raising sufficient finance to provide modern equipment to increase production and provide reasonable remuneration to those employed.

With the miners' representatives it was quite a different story. They made it clear beyond doubt that now that the industry was to be publicly owned a number of items, included in what was described as the Miners' Charter, should be immediately implemented. In the course of two conferences, after prolonged discussion, I had to remind them that improvements either in wages or in conditions of labour would be a matter for the proposed National Coal Board. The mines would not be publicly owned until the legislation had been submitted to Parliament and carried through all its stages. To which they responded, 'Unless several of the items contained in the Charter are implemented immediately, or at any rate assurances given that they will be brought into operation at an early stage, you will not get the coal you want.'

After my appointment as Minister I had addressed several meetings in the coalmining areas and gave assurances that the legislation we proposed would remove much of the discontent that existed in mining communities. Some of the miners' leaders took advantage of those assurances and asked me to receive a deputation. I readily agreed and among those who came to see me were Sir William Lawther, Sam Watson, James Bowman and Arthur Horner, the latter a member of the Communist Party. They presented me with a twelve-page charter which included a five-day week, increased rations for miners, higher wages, two weeks' holiday within the current year, and a number of other proposed reforms which, they insisted, were urgently required if sufficient coal was likely to be produced. I repeated my assurances, but made what might have been regarded as an obvious point, that the mines were still in the possession of the coalowners, and any reforms which were urgently required must be implemented in negotiations with the existing owners. Moreover, existing agreements had not expired. I had no authority to introduce any reforms, apart from items relating to health and safety in the mines, until the proposed legislation was carried through both Houses of Parliament.

The miners' leaders were adamant and expressed themselves in the strongest terms, which left no doubt in my mind that it was unlikely that coal production would be increased unless their demands were met. Two conferences were held in 1946 and in both I made it clear that I would expect the future Coal Board, acting as a public Corporation, to give these demands their attention; but, until it came into existence, I was powerless. Time and time again I was met by the threat, 'Unless these reforms emerge you will not get the coal.' To have made that statement public would have proved disastrous not only for myself, personally, but also for the Labour Party and the Government. So, during the period following those two conferences until the legislation had passed through all its stages in Parliament I was under a constant threat that the necessary quantity of coal would not be forthcoming. It was a most unenviable situation, but clearly impossible to make public.

After my transfer later from the Ministry of Fuel and Power to the War Office I asked the Ministry of Fuel and Power to make available to me the two Conference Reports. They declined on the ground that reports of that character could not be published because of the Official Secrets Act. When later on I decided, at the request of a publisher, to write a book about my experiences I sought again the use of those Conference Reports. Again I was refused. I then decided to approach the Prime Minister in power at the time, Harold Macmillan, and asked for his aid which was readily provided in the form of a room in the Treasury Offices, Great George Street, with copies of the reports made available. His help was much appreciated.

A Minister often finds himself involved in problems of this character. Some high-ranking Civil Servants appear to be a law unto themselves. My only further comment on this subject is that as an MP for an exclusively mining community it would have been invidious to have made these facts known to the public.

Of all those miners' leaders with whom I had to deal at that time only one created a favourable impression on my mind and that, strange as it may seem, was Arthur Horner, a member of the Communist Party. Indeed, I was so much impressed by his attitude and moderation that when it was my responsibility to appoint members of the first National Coal Board I asked him to become one of the members. At first he acquiesced, but later on, after a discussion he had with Harry Pollitt, the leader of the Communist Party, decided to refuse my invitation.

In 1918 the Labour Party held its Annual Conference, and among other items of proposed legislation, on the assumption that some day they would become the government of the country, they considered a formula prepared by Sidney Webb, the famous economist and social reformer, which included the transfer to public ownership of the key privately owned industries, as essential in order to improve the economy of the nation. Now, more than a quarter of a century later, I had the privilege, and venture to describe it as a distinction, of piloting the nationalisation of the coalmining industry through the House of Commons in all its stages. Regrettably, it has not succeeded in fulfilling all my expectations, in particular my desire to provide opportunities for those employed in the industry to be consulted not only on matters relating to safety, wages and working conditions, but also to share in administration and organisation of this key industry. I introduced a provision in the legislation for public ownership which would have made it possible for miners' leaders or any other representatives of the mining community to be fully consulted. But apart from the provision of pit committees, which exercise no great authority, what I had hoped for remains unfulfilled.

Participation in the administration of our industries has gained the support of both employers and many trade union leaders, though several obstacles, particularly due to suspicion on the workers' side that effective partnership would not be implemented, and on the employers' side that the presence of trade union representatives on Boards of Directors might prove embarrassing, have frustrated the efforts of those engaged in industry to regard workers' participation as eminently desirable. In this connection I quote my observations during one of the two conferences with miners' leaders in 1946 which, if acceptable, would have provided an effective partnership between the miners and the National Coal Board.

Now that we have had the preliminary enquiry I would like to proceed further and ask if you would now appoint three persons from your own side who, with some members of my staff and the association of designate members of the future Coal Board, will discuss these matters further and then report to me. I am not waiting until the Board is definitely constituted in order to prepare the ground. It is necessary to proceed quickly and the designate members of the Board are being asked to prepare plans to consider the whole position with the industry, and they have agreed to this all on the assumption that the Bill will become an Act of Parliament and they will be definitely constituted as a National Coal Board. They are going to be — I am not going to use the term employers — one of the partners in this industry. In a moment or two I shall tell you why I use the term 'partners'. They will be responsible for the general administration of the industry. And if that is to be their position several months hence it is just as well, having regard to their responsibility, that they should be brought into these discussions at once. In such a committee you come in and discuss matters freely, get all the facts and make your report to me. Then I can take some action; I do not know, I cannot commit myself to anything at this stage. It would be wrong of me to do so, but at any rate that is the course of action which I think ought to be pursued.

I said a moment or two ago that I would tell you why I use the term 'partners' in connection with the National Coal Board. I have now put on the Order Paper of the House my new clause which provides for consultation in the industry. I think you will find it satisfactory. I do not think we can go any further than we have done. It provides for consultation between the National Union of Mineworkers and other organisations associated with the ancillary industries, not exclusively about wages and labour conditions or health, safety and welfare which are all essential, but it goes beyond that; on any matter of mutual concern you are coming into the discussions as partners in this great enterprise, discussing the organisation plans and everything else that pertains to the future of the industry along with the members of the Coal Board. That is a great transformation, and if it is accepted by the Committee and by the House of Commons eventually, as we expect it will be because I intend to force it through, and would even be prepared to consider amendments in order to strengthen it, if necessary. If that is done you will have a completely new situation in the coal industry.

I should have expected the miners' leaders to have immediately agreed to what was likely to produce a new situation in the industry. As part of the partnership proposed they were offered two seats on the National Coal Board, but they refused, saying that administration was not their affair. I was disappointed when Will Lawther, the leader of the delegation, said, 'Mr Minister, can we bring you back to where we started in all these discussions and proceed to demand the immediate application of reforms', which I had no power to authorise and which, in the ordinary course, would be the subject of negotiations.

Let me make here a general comment on nationalisation. When members of the Party use as one of their regular slogans, 'Abolish Capitalism', they must have regard to the alternative. If the State is responsible for the ownership, policy and supervision of public services and intervenes when considered necessary, we must ensure that every effort is made to avoid some of the problems that have been associated with public ownership. I will not accept that even the nationalised coal industry is consistent in structure and operations with Socialism. There are as many class distinctions and gradations in status, class and salaries in the nationalised coal industry as are to be found in Capitalist society. They have their bosses, only with other names. Doubtless the mining community has gained by public ownership. Improved working conditions, higher wages, more security; but if this is what is accepted as Socialism, I decline to endorse it. Almost the same could be said about British Rail, nationalised steel, Civil Aviation and even the Bank of England. In short, Socialism is as much an attitude of mind as essential variations are in the mechanism of industry.

Meanwhile, I was faced with remarkable absenteeism in most coalmining areas and, to my regret, particularly in my own constituency of Easington where we had from 18 to 20 per cent absenteeism. Generally speaking, ex-miners, many of whom had either worked in munition factories or were in the Forces, refused to return to the mines.

14

At the War Office

Among my responsibilities as Minister of Fuel and Power was the provision of electricity supply and also oil. Concerning the latter I received information from our representative in Iran, at that time our main source of supply, that both the Soviet Union and private interests in the United States were operating in affairs concerning oil production to our disadvantage. I considered it was my duty to convey this information to the Foreign Secretary and, simultaneously, to submit the information I had received from our official representative about maladministration affecting the coalfields in the Ruhr in Germany, over which, at the time, we exercised control. Not a single sentence in my letter to Ernest Bevin contained any personal criticism. That was never my intention; it would have been disloyal. My purpose was solely to furnish information in the expectation that the Foreign Secretary would submit it to the Prime Minister and, if necessary, subsequently to the Cabinet. No reply was received from the Foreign Office, and on consultation with my principal officials I decided it was not for me to take further action. What happened as a result of my communication to the Foreign Secretary was never disclosed to me. I learnt something some years later when I obtained a copy of Attlee's memoirs, in which a letter from the Foreign Secretary had described my submission as an intervention in his affairs, but strangely enough the information contained in my letter to Bevin does not appear. I can only assume that some aspects of foreign policy were conducted in secret between Bevin and Attlee. No submission came before the Cabinet.

While attending a Cabinet Meeting a message came that the Tory Opposition on the Standing Committee on mines nationalisation had made a vigorous attack on the Government and I was asked to go hurriedly to the meeting, which I did. Having heard what had happened, I responded by making a vigorous reply. Evidently my language was not to the liking of the Government Whip, a miners' MP, who reported it to the Chief Whip, who reported it to the Prime Minister. I was accused of fomenting trouble: creating controversy when I should, by more modest behaviour, have permitted the Opposition to abuse the Government! I suspect this MP from a coal-mining area would have liked my job!

However, despite the pressure either for my transfer or dismissal from office, several months elapsed before Attlee took any action. Then he sent for me in October 1947, six months after the so-called crisis, and said it was his intention that the Ministry of Fuel and Power should no longer be represented in the Cabinet. 'We have,' he said, 'discharged our obligation and carried the Nationalisation Bill through the House of Commons with success through all its stages.' It was now on the Statute Book. Despite the criticism, he added, we were now producing more coal and, therefore, while a Minister should be appointed for the Department, he ought not to be in the Cabinet. Thus Hugh Gaitskell, who was Parliamentary Secretary, became the Minister, not in the Cabinet, and Attlee suggested I should go to the War Office as Secretary of State.

I immediately declined and proposed to return to the back benches. Attlee would have none of it. He had already, in his constituency, made a public declaration: 'What had occurred in the so-called fuel crisis,' he said, 'was a matter for the Cabinet, who must accept the responsibility, and not the Minister; that should be enough.' Despite this, I continued with my refusal and arranged to take my belongings from the Department and go to the back benches, but my Parliamentary Private Secretary, Colonel (later Lord) Wigg, who had always displayed the utmost loyalty, intervened, and sought the aid of Harold Laski, who at the time was Chairman of the Labour Party, to intercede and persuade me to accept the invitation. Wigg was furious with me and said, 'Why do you refuse to accept an office of this kind? It is an honourable office. It is an important appointment.' He was so vigorous and aggressive about it as almost to disturb our friendship. As a result I decided to accept the invitation and informed the Prime Minister accordingly.

Having been transferred from the Ministry of Fuel and Power to the War Office, 'to the surprise of everybody' (not my language) I became a success, as I did later at the Ministry of Defence. Why were people surprised? Was it because I was regarded as incompetent, or was there some other defect? Had I misbehaved? Attlee himself never expressed surprise. Why did Francis Williams, who collaborated with Attlee in writing his memoirs, offer an opinion in the book on who had expressed surprise that I was a success? Was I to regard this as a compliment? Was it suggested by a Cabinet colleague? We may never know. But why had we to wait for Attlee's memoirs several years after the event to learn the truth?

When I went to the War Office I was informed by General Browning, otherwise known in the office as 'Boy Browning', who was the Military Secretary, 'The Generals won't have you.' To his surprise I was able to reply, 'That is remarkable; I have just received a letter from General Montgomery expressing his pleasure at my appointment and extending a warm welcome.'

It is interesting to note that when later I returned to the Cabinet, as Minister of Defence, and was about to leave the War Office, General Steele, the Adjutant General, came to me and said, 'When you came here two years ago we were going to resign, and now that you are leaving us we feel like resigning.' I hope that comment will satisfy some of my critics.

I must make it quite clear that if in the course of my observations I appear to indulge in criticism of some people, let it be understood that in my Parliamentary life, though knocked about time and time again, I have never whined or cried about it. I attack whenever it is necessary; I am ready to endure criticism if, in the opinion of others, I deserve it.

As an indication of my reception when I went to the War Office, here is the letter I received from General Montgomery, then Chief of the Imperial General Staff:

Dear Mr. Shinwell,

Welcome to the War Office, I look forward to working with you.

Yours sincerely,
Montgomery of Alamein.

140

During my term of office at the Department, when Montgomery was, to use his own language, transformed into an international soldier as Chairman of the Brussels Military Treaty Organisation, we were on the most friendly terms. However, while still a member of the Cabinet as Minister of Fuel and Power I had heard rumours that Montgomery was at loggerheads with the then Minister of Defence, A.V. Alexander, and had also engaged in some controversy with Ernest Bevin, the Foreign Secretary, including some indiscreet references to the Government. When, after some delay and advice by my colleague, George Wigg, disturbed because of my reluctance to go to the War Office, I decided to inform the Prime Minister that I accepted the invitation, my unwillingness was largely due to Montgomery's reputation and temperament. My opinions were confirmed when Montgomery published his memoirs and I learned that the rumours of disagreement between Monty and some members of the Government were substantiated. Since then I am convinced that in view of the controversies and disagreements contained in Monty's memoirs, it was not at all unlikely that I might, in going to the War Office, have been similarly involved. To quote from Montgomery's memoirs, however relevant, would occupy too much space. The relevant pages are 474 and 483 to 488, and the memoirs are available in most libraries. However, I take the liberty of expressing my suspicions as follows.

When the Foreign Secretary complained that he had been 'let down by the Army' Montgomery got very angry and demanded that such an insult should be withdrawn. Monty reported the incident to his colleagues and later asked the Minister of Defence if the Foreign Secretary had 'withdrawn his insult to the Army'. The Minister of Defence said, 'There was no need to worry; the remark had not been made in public.' To which Monty replied that the Army knew all about it, and became so angry that, to use his own language, 'he went right off the deep end'. Indeed, Montgomery was so disturbed that he said, 'If the Government want to sack me it would be OK by me. I could say a jugful in the House of Lords about the Government's handling of the Palestine situation and would be delighted to have the opportunity to do so.' The Field Marshal certainly did not pull his punches in his discussions either with the Minister of

Defence or the Foreign Secretary, and what emerged from the discussions, the interrogations and angry exchanges, confirms my suspicions that some of my colleagues in the Cabinet would have been delighted if similar experiences had occurred when I became Secretary for War and Minister of Defence. How disappointed must they have felt when they learned, and I quote not my own expression but what appears elsewhere from an authoritative source, 'everybody was surprised' that I had 'become such a success'.

In face of this evidence, and in view of the pressure exerted by Dalton, Stafford Cripps and other members of the Labour Party to have me removed from the Cabinet, my reluctance, when George Wigg spoke about the War Office being an honourable appointment, was not due to any antipathy towards our Forces, but because I suspected that there was a conspiracy against me and naturally resented it at the time. On the available evidence my suspicions are emphatically confirmed. Why transfer me to the War Office, knowing by temperament, and aware of Monty's disagreements with Alexander, Minister of Defence, with Ernest Bevin, Foreign Secretary, and even critical of the Prime Minister? Did they, with the exception of Attlee, come to the conclusion, those loyal colleagues of mine, that by sending me to the War Office in the expectation of even more controversy and disagreement it would be the end of me, either by resignation or dismissal from office? I wonder.

I am unable to say that my experience at the Ministry of Fuel and Power was altogether a happy one. I was encircled by opponents of nationalisation; not, I agree, the principal Civil Servants — most were first class — but the attitude of some officials. I quote two examples. When I went to Millbank as Minister of Fuel and Power I was asked by the Permanent Under-Secretary whether I cared to make a choice of Private Secretaries. I asked him to introduce a few of them to me for my selection. There was an occasion when I asked one of the Private Secretaries for some information about the cost of my personal correspondence and, quite innocently, asked for advice about my postage. This official, with obvious superiority and sarcasm, said, 'You are now a rich man.' It was difficult for me to make a reply to this somewhat inappropriate observation, but when a Civil Servant can speak in such a fashion to a

Minister it is an indication that there exists a difference of attitude, possibly of a political or maybe a social character.

On another occasion a question was put on the Order Paper in the House of Commons, asking me for a forecast of electricity consumption. I asked the appropriate official of my Department to furnish me with a statistical reply, which he did, and this I gave to the MP who asked the question, only to discover a week later that my information was misleading, and so I informed the House accordingly; but, naturally, I failed, conforming to tradition, to mention that it was the fault of the Civil Servant upon whose information I was bound to rely. Even in the height and displeasure associated with what was described as a fuel crisis (which we have since discovered, both in Attlee's memoirs and in Cabinet records, was no crisis at all) there was slender evidence of encouragement for the Minister. It is impossible to present an understandable comparison as between the two Departments. All I say is that in contrast to my experience at the Ministry of Fuel and Power, I found my experience at the War Office and Ministry of Defence congenial, with many problems but ample evidence of co-operation and, indeed, even enthusiasm of both Civil Servants and the military personnel in all sections of my Department.

As Minister of Defence I naturally made several visits overseas; to Europe to watch manoeuvres, to visit members of the Forces, all of which I found most pleasant and informative. However, I encountered one problem: that was when I was asked to go to Washington in company with two generals who were weapon experts to deal with the controversial issue as to which was the best modern rifle in production. The British had made such a claim; so had the Americans and the Belgians. We in the United Kingdom had also produced not only what we regarded as the best rifle in the world, but also the most appropriate ammunition. I was not sent to Washington because I possessed expert knowledge: that was for the experts; but I could, in the opinion of the Prime Minister, be more articulate, and he relied to a large extent on my debating skill, having to face some formidable opposition. General Collins, who presided and represented the USA, treated me with the utmost courtesy. For five days we argued, sometimes without enmity or any desire to be controversial, but on other occasions with

143

vigour and, at the end, opposition. Despite all the arguments adduced by the representatives of the other countries involved, I refused to yield. I pleaded and argued with such knowledge as I possessed, encouraged my assistants to act in similar vein, and after five days of negotiation made it clear beyond doubt that in my opinion our weapon was the best yet produced.

On the day following the conclusion of our proceedings I went to New York to catch my plane for London. Before leaving I was accosted by some Pressmen who asked me to furnish them with a report of our deliberations and the reason why I had maintained that the British weapon was the best. I gave them reasons not unlike those, though somewhat more brief, that I had advanced in Washington. And then, to my surprise, they suggested that as I had apparently become very popular, even among the Opposition in Washington, I should after my activities remain for a few days. I expressed thanks, but informed them that I must return to London on the way to my constituency. Was this so important, they asked. I assured them it was. I had, for round about thirty years, judged the annual beauty contest associated with my constituency and neighbourhood and, therefore, must return. On the following Monday I was in my constituency, judging the contest to an audience of at least 50,000 in the open air, and about a week later I received a copy of an American newspaper with a story relating to my decision with the suggestion that 'Mr Shinwell preferred legs to arms'!

The comment underlines an important difference between a British Cabinet Minister and his American counterpart. A British Minister is also a Member of Parliament, and as such still concerned with local matters in his constituency as well as with matters of national importance. He is sometimes in a dilemma, torn between his national duties and his obligations towards his constituents. Those obligations may be of a social character and appear trivial, but they matter to the voters who elected him. In retrospect, as leader of the British delegation in Washington stating the case for British weapons, I did my duty for 'arms', and in my constituency for 'legs'.

A.V. Alexander, when Minister of Defence in the Attlee Government, was subjected to considerable criticism, as was the Government, for continuing National Service. In the opin-

(*Top*) As Chairman of the Labour Party Conference, Scarborough, 1947. Ernest Bevin is speaking; I am sitting on his right.

(*Bottom*) Prime Minister Attlee addressing Government colleagues on the success of mines nationalisation in January 1947. I am in the chair.

(*Above*) 'Shinwell's Shovel': during the 'coal crisis' my popularity lay with those workers who sought to help transport coal with various vehicles.

(*Left*) Speaking at Murton, County Durham in 1947 when the nationalisation of mines legislation was carried.

(*Right*) A welcome from General Crocker, Commander in the Middle East, when, as Secretary for War, I visited the forces.

(*Below*) A conference in New York, 1950. From left to right: Ernest Bevin, myself, Robert Schuman, Jules Moch, Dean Atcheson, General George C. Marshall.

The marriage to my second wife, Dinah, a wonderful and highly intelligent woman.

(*Opposite above*) Posing with three of my grandchildren: Michael, now a London financial expert, David, now a book publisher in Australia, and John, now a captain in the Merchant Navy.

(*Opposite below*) 'Shinwell prefers legs to arms,' suggests the American press when I hurry home from a conference on weapons in Washington to judge the annual beauty contest in County Durham.

(*Right*) Speaking at the Savoy Hotel to raise funds for a children's hospital.

(*Below*) At the age of ninety—with a sense of humour, but also inclined to look pugnacious.

(*Left*) On a visit to Israel: Sarah, my third wife, and I with Golda Meir, a great friend.

(*Below*) Being awarded an honorary DCL at Durham University, 1969.

(*Left*) Sponsoring the Admiral of the Fleet, Lord Hill Norton, in the House of Lords—an honour to do so, in my opinion, for there are not many men like this great military expert.

(*Below*) At home aged ninety-five; not relaxing so much as reflecting—so much to think about, so many questions unanswered.

ion of Montgomery and other Chiefs of Staff, in view of the international tension and the possibility of conflict emerging in Europe, in addition to the Communist trouble in Malaysia, it was necessary that men should be retained, and those who were conscripted for service should serve a minimum of eighteen months. Under pressure, largely from the pacifist section of the Labour Party, Alexander was forced to give way and reluctantly agreed to twelve months instead of eighteen months' service. This infuriated the Chiefs of Staff who were convinced that it was impossible to train men efficiently and make them fit for service overseas in twelve months, and therefore, after considerable discussion and further disagreements, Alexander was forced by MPs to abandon the idea of twelve months and return to the original suggestion advanced by the military of eighteen months. These oscillations about the length of military service also concerned the Foreign Secretary, Ernest Bevin, who was himself apprehensive of disturbance in Europe. In consequence, when I became Minister of Defence and returned to the Cabinet in 1950, and the trouble in Malaysia had become more critical, we decided to send General Templar (later Field-Marshal) to Malaysia with full authority to promote a settlement. Templar was selected not only for his knowledge of military strategy, but also because he was regarded as a political general, capable of solving problems with diplomatic skill.

My first important speech as Minister of Defence took place on a Motion of 14 February 1951 asking the House to approve the Defence Policy of the Government. The speech is much too long to quote. It was fully reported in the national Press at the time. I shall only mention two items to demonstrate that the international situation today is similar to that to which I referred during my speech in 1951, almost thirty years ago.

In a reference to NATO I stated that the organisation had been transformed from a military planning body into an effective defence organisation for the North Atlantic area. Our intention was to provide the means of building up forces strong enough to deter the potential aggressor more rapidly and successfully than seemed at one time possible, provided that all the member countries fulfilled the tasks they had agreed to undertake. To this I added:

It cannot be said too often that there is nothing aggressive in what we are doing, with due regard to the military organisation and tremendous forces available to Soviet Russia and her satellites, probably the largest and most formidable forces ever maintained by any country in peacetime. We have no intention of making war on anybody but, on the other hand, if we fail to strengthen our own defences, in a world where others are arming with great speed and with modern weapons, we shall invite attack. Nothing would give the Government greater satisfaction than to be able to say that all other countries have demonstrated their desire to settle differences peacefully.

To ensure that men were properly prepared for service in the area it was essential to provide adequate training, and I personally held the view, expressed to my military assistants at the time, that eighteen months would be short of what was required. It would take from six to nine months to train a man for guerrilla and jungle warfare, having regard to weather conditions and the state of affairs in Malaysia at that time, keep him on active service for at least another six months, and also provide ample time for his return to the United Kingdom and, if necessary, to civil life. Eventually, despite Parliamentary criticism to which I was subjected as one might expect, the two-year principle was accepted, but not without political and personal consequences. One was that at the succeeding Labour Party Conference, held in Morecambe, the opponents of my views — and, indeed, of military expenditure of any kind — were organised and succeeded in removing me from my membership of the Labour Party Executive, of which I had been for some years a member and also Chairman. This manoeuvre was most efficiently organised. Indeed, one prominent Parliamentarian, Ian Mikardo, described by some people as the Parliamentary Bookmaker, accepted several bets on whether or not I could be rejected from the Executive. In my place Mrs Barbara Castle was appointed.

I learned with interest that at the Labour Party Conference held in 1978 Ian Mikardo lost his seat on the National Executive. I can imagine how he felt. I can assure all and sundry, including the victim, that I had nothing to do with the organisation which caused his defeat!

146

15

The MacArthur Controversy

Naturally I was pleased to return to the Cabinet and to occupy the most important post of Minister of Defence. Not that I was unhappy at the War Office; it was an informative and agreeable experience. Never during my period of office as Secretary of State for War did I fail to obtain the co-operation of my military colleagues of all ranks and the Civil Service. I am bound to repeat, though regretfully, that my experience at the War Office was in marked contrast to that at the Ministry of Fuel and Power where my responsibilities and problems were enlarged by what appeared to be an absence of co-operation. This, of course, I emphasise, does not apply to the principal Civil Servants at the Ministry, though I am aware of their doubts about nationalisation, but applies more to those of lower rank.

The first problem I had to tackle at the Ministry of Defence was that of pay and pensions for the Forces. This was a vexatious problem that had disturbed previous governments and in particular my predecessor. I decided to consult the Chiefs of Staff and the Permanent Secretary of the Ministry, and after extensive enquiry we reached the conclusion that it was essential to improve the financial conditions of all ranks in the Forces. Naturally, our views were conveyed to the Treasury, and Hugh Gaitskell, as Chancellor of the Exchequer, requested a consultation with me on the subject. Somewhat to my surprise, instead of asking me to call at the Treasury he decided to come to my office. This I assume was out of courtesy because he had been my junior as Parliamentary Secretary when I was Minister of Fuel and Power; I appreciated his action. I required a minimum sum of fifty-five million pounds as an advance which, though it might not prove completely satisfactory, would go some way to improve conditions. He considered the sum required was excessive so we failed to agree, and eventually I decided I must go to the Cabinet and ask my colleagues to make the decision. I was fortunate in gaining considerable support from a majority of Cabinet colleagues, led by Dr Addison, later Viscount Addison, despite Treasury opposition, and eventually obtained a unanimous decision for the full amount.

Another problem of a more awkward character emerged from the United States decision to provide forces to assist the South Koreans in their conflict with the North; we were informed that China would be involved. In the absence of endorsement from the United Nations we were reluctant to support the United States, but, because of apprehension of further conflict, I decided after consultation with the Chiefs of Staff to hold our contribution available if and when the United Nations endorsed the decision of the USA. Meanwhile, trade between the United Kingdom and China was developing, and questions were asked in the House of Commons about the effect of our exports to that country. This, however, was not a matter for my Department, but the responsibility of the Board of Trade, whose Minister was Hartley Shawcross. Eventually we completed our preparations for the despatch of Land Forces to the area, together with one of our warships, the *Theseus*, to operate off-shore. If I refer to this matter in the context of my activities I make no apology because of the valour and sacrifice of our Land Forces, in particular of the Gloucester Regiment, who, outnumbered at Seoul, were completely wiped out. Their exploits and the sacrifice involved are to the credit of the British Army.

I was called upon to answer questions in Parliament and report the activities of our Forces and their operations from day to day. A complete account of the conflict is contained in the Parliamentary Report, including my speech as Minister, but I content myself with emphasising my respect and admiration for the valiant services rendered by our Land Forces. However, I received a rude shock when Winston Churchill initiated a debate on the export of various commodities to China which he contended would be used to the disadvantage of both the American and the British Forces. In the course of one speech he referred to a statement I made about the possibility of peace when General MacArthur, in charge of the American Forces, was likely to be removed. By this time the Prime Minister, Clem Attlee, had warned the American Government about the possibility of General MacArthur making an attack on the Chinese border, which would have involved us in a far more serious conflict. Churchill having referred to the subject, I ventured to interrupt him and declared he misunderstood what I had said. I quote the Parliamentary Report about what happened and also almost in full the speech I made the following day in a personal statement which completely destroyed Churchill's allegations. In his reply to my speech he grudgingly agreed that he had misunderstood the statement I made about General MacArthur.

Mr. Churchill: . . . Our advice to the Government is to stop rubber entirely now and to reach an agreement with the United States on the general question of trade with China in a spirit which will make the United States feel that their cause is our cause, and that we mean at all costs to be good friends and allies. I read with emotion the testimony of General Marshall before the Senate Committee — [Interruption.] The right hon. Gentleman had better take a back seat: well, he has done so.

The Minister of Defence (Mr. Shinwell) rose—

Mr. Churchill: It is quite right that the right hon. Gentleman should take a back seat. He made a statement the other day about no appeasement and so on. I was glad to read it, but he had spoiled it all before and by the remark he made at a most disturbing moment in the United States, that now, perhaps, things will go better in Korea, once General MacArthur had been dismissed. If anything—

Mr. Shinwell rose—

Hon. Members: Withdraw. [This was addressed to Churchill.]

Mr. Churchill: Hon. Members will not frighten me by their yelling. If anything could at that time have got about fifty million Americans furious with him, and with the Government for whom he spoke, it would have been to use language like that. I am very glad that he tried to undo the harm he did by making his speech against appeasement.

Mr. Shinwell: The right hon. Gentleman has just asserted that I declared that the dismissal of General MacArthur should be brought about because it would be of advantage to us. [Hon. Members: 'No'] Let me tell the right hon. Gentleman that the statement which he has just made, in which he alleges that I made that statement about General MacArthur, is utterly false, and I challenge the right hon. Gentleman to produce the written evidence or withdraw. I challenge him in this House to produce the written evidence that I made a statement similar to what he has just said.

Mr. Churchill: I understood, from what was reported in the Press —

Mr. Shinwell: Which Press?

Mr. Churchill: — that the right hon. Gentleman said that perhaps things will now go better in Korea since General MacArthur had been removed.

Mr. Shinwell: Let me tell the right hon. Gentleman that I never made any such statement. I challenge him to produce that statement.

Hon. Members: Withdraw.

Mr. Churchill: No, I would not think of withdrawing. I will produce the newspaper report on which I base myself. I have not got it in my notes at the moment, but I will get it. I thought it a most unfortunate statement.

Mr. Shinwell: I never made that statement.

Mr. Churchill: We shall be very glad to hear what was the statement which the right hon. Gentleman actually made. It is always part of the tactics to throw the blame on to the Press, and so on. However, I will produce the Press reports which I read on the subject, and I think they were pretty widely noted. Of course, nobody wishes to accuse the Minister of Defence of crimes which he has not committed.

Mr Shinwell rose —

Hon. Members: Sit down.

Mr. Shinwell: I shall not sit down. May I tell the right hon. Gentleman that he has made a most false statement about me in this

House, and that he has no right to make such statements about
Ministers?

Mr. Churchill: Do not be so nervous about it.

Mr. Shinwell: I am not nervous about it. [Laughter.] You should be
ashamed of yourself. The right hon. Gentleman has done more
harm to this country than anyone. [This reference applied solely to
the Korean affair.]

On the day following the above debate I made a personal
statement:

Mr. Shinwell: With your permission, Sir Charles, and with that of
the Committee, I should like to make a personal statement. In the
course of the speech by the right hon. Gentleman the Member for
Woodford (Mr. Churchill) I interrupted him because of some
disagreement with what he said. My impression of what he said was
that I am alleged to have said — the right hon. Gentleman will
correct me if I am wrong in that impression — something calculated
to discredit General MacArthur. That was my impression. I
resented it because I could not remind myself of anything that I had
said which was derogatory to the General.

The right hon. Gentlemen was good enough to convey to me a
report from *The Times* of 23rd April. However, in the statement
which the right hon. Gentleman made, he appeared to have over-
looked the context of the setting in which the speech was made and
the matter with which I was dealing. Perhaps I may have the
permission of the Committee to read a rather longer extract from
the *New York Times* of 23rd April. The heading of their report is,
'Shinwell optimistic on outlook in Korea.' It states:

'Defence Minister Emanuel Shinwell said today that the removal
of General of the Army Douglas MacArthur gave the United
Nations and representatives of the Chinese Communist Government a new chance to negotiate peace in Korea.'

That was the subject with which I was dealing. The report continued:

'Addressing his constituents here, Mr. Shinwell said:
  It might be that with the removal of General MacArthur from
  the Korean atmosphere, conditions may improve, but we

cannot tell. I am bound to say that I regret that the Peiping Government is not more responsive to the suggestions that have been made to negotiate peace in Korea.

I think that opportunity has been present for some considerable time, but here again is the opportunity for the United Nations representatives and the representatives of the Peiping Government to gather together to bring this Korean affair to an end." '

That was the statement I made and my submission is that there is nothing in that statement that was derogatory to General MacArthur. Certainly, there was nothing I said which seemed to imply that I was casting some doubt on the capacity of General MacArthur to conduct military operations, because that was not in my mind. I was dealing exclusively with the prospect of re-opening negotiations with a view to promoting the peace through the United Nations in Korea. And *The Times* report, a somewhat shorter report, I should imagine conveys the same impression.

It may be that my impression of what the right hon. Gentleman said to me, or about me, was wrong, and if so I ask that I should be forgiven for gaining a wrong impression. On the other hand, it may be that the right hon. Gentleman, having seen the shorter report, thought I had said something which was calculated both to throw discredit on General MacArthur in the military sphere, and also to disturb our relations with the United States. That was indeed far from my mind.

Churchill, during the current discussions, was in his most impish and provocative mood. He enjoyed criticising the Opposition and, in particular, Members of the Cabinet, though none of his antics weakened my admiration for this remarkable man and outstanding character. I have sometimes been a victim, but have to admit to have also appreciated his magnanimity.

In the course of my activities at the Ministry of Defence the subject of expenditure could not be ignored, in particular because of the protests by some of the pacifist members of the Labour Party who wished to terminate National Service, much against the advice of Ernest Bevin, the Foreign Secretary, and protested about what they described as excessive military expenditure. I decided, instead of adopting the usual practice of annual estimates of expenditure, to provide for a three-yearly period on the ground that it would provide greater stability and also be more informative, both for Parliament and the general public. Having consulted the Chiefs of Staff and asked for estimates and requirements from the Admiralty, the War Office and the Air Ministry, I discovered that the total for the three years would be six thousand million pounds. However, remembering my experience at the War Office, I decided that what that Department was demanding was excessive, and reduced the figure to four thousand seven hundred million. This figure was accepted by the Cabinet, at first with no opposition from any member. Then the Chancellor of the Exchequer, Hugh Gaitskell, following the policy of his predecessor, Stafford Cripps, decided there must be a reduction of expenditure in the Health Services, particularly with regard to the cost to the public of teeth and spectacles. Nye Bevan, the Minister of Health, strongly protested against the Treasury proposition and threatened to resign. The matter was considered by the Cabinet at several meetings but, meanwhile, the Prime Minister was in hospital and Herbert Morrison presided at Cabinet meetings. Then, to my surprise and that of other members of the Cabinet, Nye Bevan, supported by Harold Wilson, decided to oppose the estimates for military expenditure.

I must confess that at the time there was a great deal of confusion as to which item called for the threat to resign, whether it was a reduction in the estimates for the Health Service or for military expenditure. Eventually, after a committee had been appointed to seek a compromise and failed, both Bevan and Wilson threatened to resign. By this time Nye Bevan had been transferred from his post as Minister of Health to Minister of Labour, which was regarded as a demotion. He had expected, instead of being demoted, to have been appointed either as Chancellor of the Exchequer or — owing to the death of Ernest Bevin — as Foreign Secretary. It is possible that if Attlee had been able to take part in the discussions some compromise would have been reached. However, the resignations occurred, with the result that in the subsequent General Election we were defeated and Churchill was returned as Prime Minister with a majority of sixteen.

If Bevan and Wilson had associated their resignations in

specific terms with the subject of teeth and spectacles, which was their original complaint, instead of protesting against military expenditure during a period when considerable numbers of men were being retained in the Forces because of international tension and concern about Moscow's intentions, we would not have lost the election.

16

The Bitterness of Suez

In October 1956 the Government decided to send a representative delegation of two Members, one from the House of Commons and the other from the House of Lords, to Australia with presentation to the several governments included in the federal system in celebration of their Centenary. I was appointed for the House of Commons and the Marquis of Lansdowne for the House of Lords. Just preceding our departure we were informed that President Nasser, incensed by the action of the United States and Britain, apparently connected with financial arrangements associated with the construction of the Aswan Dam, had seized the Suez Canal and made it Egyptian property. This act of nationalisation without previous negotiations was regarded as arbitrary and, indeed, in view of previous treaties, illegal. The Prime Minister, Anthony Eden, following upon demands from the Opposition for clarification, promised to make a statement which the House of Commons heard a few days later. Meanwhile, unofficial information was available to Members of both Houses about alleged collusion between Britain, France and also Israel for military action directed against Egypt.

Hugh Gaitskell, at that time Leader of the Opposition, received the announcement concerning the Suez Canal affair with calm, and while in that mood asked a series of questions while condemning President Nasser for his arbitrary action in seizing the Canal, describing him as a person 'whose ambition was to be Emperor of the Near East', but suggested that efforts in the direction of a peaceful arrangement should be set in train. It was a moderate speech, by no means critical of the Prime Minister or the Conservative Government. However, within twenty-four hours some of the Left Wing Members of the

Labour Party with strong pacifist views expressed their resentment at this moderation and demanded that if any troops were alerted for action they should be immediately withdrawn. The response was regarded as unsatisfactory, and a majority of Labour Members were almost in a state of frenzy. I am unable to recall in all my Parliamentary experience a scene so hysterical, accompanied by so much abuse, particularly by the pacifist Members of the Party, as occurred on this occasion. Meanwhile the Parliamentary Committee of the Labour Party, known as the Shadow Cabinet, had prepared a resolution which at first contained a condemnation of Israel, though there was no accurate information which justified the belief that Israel was involved, but on the representation of a few members, including myself, they decided to withdraw the reference to Israel, and even to France, and confined the resolution to an unspecified condemnation of aggression.

Before leaving the United Kingdom I had the opportunity of consulting with other Members and also with some high-ranking officers in the Army, and learned from them that General Keithley, who had served as my Military Secretary when Secretary for War, was Commander in Chief in the area involved, and had informed the Government that it was physically impossible to mount anything in the nature of an assault for at least six weeks. At that time our military base in the Middle East was at Malta. Our Egyptian base, the Canal Zone as it was called, had been abandoned some years before on the insistence of Bevin, Foreign Secretary in the Attlee 1945–51 Government, against my advice and that of our military experts. It is possible that premature withdrawal of our Forces from the Canal Zone encouraged Nasser to act as he did. I also had an opportunity of speaking with Prime Minister Eden; I must confess I found him very disturbed, apparently not quite sure which direction to take. It seemed from our brief conversation, confirmed later by more accurate information, that the Cabinet members were divided; some were in favour of accepting the situation and hoping for a compromise, others were supporting the Prime Minister in alerting the Forces which seemed available.

Controversy on the facts of British intentions and even our capabilities has never ceased, so I make no further comment on that aspect, but I had much to say in the course of many speeches I made in the various Australian States, and later in New Zealand, when, after my Australian visit, I decided to proceed under my own steam and at my own expense, and during my way back to the UK, when I took an opportunity of speaking to several influential people in San Francisco. I ventured to express my conviction that Eden was less to blame, despite the criticism levelled against him, than was either Eisenhower or Dulles who had both given assurances to the Egyptian Government of financial assistance, in co-operation with the United Kingdom, in connection with the Aswan Dam and had then withdrawn them, thus paving the way for the arbitrary action by Nasser which had almost created a serious conflict in the Middle East.

During my absence from the UK I learned from the Australian and New Zealand Press that our people at home were deeply divided on the issue, including some Members of Parliament, even my own colleagues, who, for some reason, had sought to provoke the Labour Executive in my constituency of Easington to condemn me for the speeches I had made, and demanded my return. On receipt of a cable from my Executive I replied that I would return according to the schedule arranged and, some weeks later, when there was rather more calm and tranquillity than the previous circumstances warranted, I met my Executive, gave my explanation, condemned Nasser and upheld Anthony Eden, except for the expression that one should not enter into a quarrel without being prepared, and left the court without a stain on my character. Two considerations were uppermost, that my constituency supported me, and that I did what was right.

My official itinerary had been confined to Australia. My intention was, and arrangements were made for me, to stay in Wellington with the Governor General, but when I arrived in Auckland I was informed that Prince Philip was occupying the guest room so I had to wait until it was vacated. Consequently, instead of going to Wellington, I was advised to go to Rotorua where the Hot Springs are, described then as a health resort. After a six-hour bus journey I arrived and stayed at a hotel. Later, after making arrangements about my accommodation, I went for a walk. Rotorua was much more primitive then than it is now. On another visit, fifteen years later, what I saw would justify describing it, in comparison to what it was on my first visit, as a paradise. As I walked along the streets on my first visit the vapour was bursting out of the ground almost everywhere. I didn't care much for it, so next morning went down to the travel office and asked them to arrange a reservation at Wellington at some hotel. My purpose was to stay there for a few days and then go to the Governor General's residence. I also went to the office of the airways company, and arranged an air flight to Wellington, which was about three hundred miles away.

I went back to the hotel, packed my bag, paid my bill and then sat in the garden. I had some time to wait before my taxi arrived. Then I saw an elderly man throwing some kind of mixture on a bed of roses. At that time, in my house in Hampstead Garden Suburb, I had a beautiful garden with a vast number of rose bushes, and was therefore interested. 'What is that mixture you are throwing on the roses?' I asked. For a moment or two he paid no attention. Then he looked round and in a strong Scottish accent said, 'Just a mixture.' I said, 'You are a Scotsman. How long have you been in New Zealand?' 'Forty years,' he replied. 'You haven't lost your accent,' I said. He paid very little attention to my remark, but then turned and said, 'Aye, what about it?' I thought I would pursue the conversation and said, 'I think I know where you come from.' Again, rather indifferently, he said, 'Where do I come from?' I said, 'You come from a place between Glasgow and Edinburgh, probably Polmont or Falkirk.' 'No,' he said, 'but you are gey near it.' 'Well, where do you come from?' I asked. He replied, 'I come from Whitburn.' 'Do you know I once represented Whitburn in the House of Commons when I sat for Linlithgow,' I said. Again he paid no attention, almost ignored me. Then he turned and said, 'What's your name?' What could I do? I had started the conversation about roses, so in a very muted tone of voice said, 'Shinwell.' This time he completely ignored me, and then suddenly he almost jumped up and shouted, 'You were a wild man in those days.' Fortunately, my taxi came and I took my case and said goodbye. As I went out of the hotel gate he said, 'I'll aye remember you and what you said.'

What do I remember about Whitburn? It was a small town in

West Lothian. It was Conservative; very much so. Someone there called Harvie Watt used to heckle me. Now he is a most important industrial tycoon. He gave me more trouble than anybody else. At one meeting I nearly had a fight with him. Some years later he became a Member of the House of Commons and was engaged as Churchill's Parliamentary Private Secretary. During the Second World War, when I intervened in most debates, we became quite friendly and he would come and ask, particularly when we were going into secret session, if I proposed to speak so he could inform his Chief. On one occasion he came to me when we were expecting a row about the condition of our tanks which were regarded by some military experts as inadequate, and asked if I was going to take part in the debate. I told him, 'No. I think a case can be made out, but I don't want in the present situation to indulge in criticism of the Government. But,' I said, 'if I do speak I might say some harsh things about your Chief because he has some responsibility. He should have known about the tank defects.' He became angry, and said, 'Don't talk about my Chief in that fashion. He is a great military expert,' then added, 'what's more, a descendant of the Duke of Marlborough, the greatest of our military experts.' I couldn't let that pass. 'Don't talk to me about his great military ancestors. Who do you think you are talking to? Do you know who my ancestor was?' He said, 'No. Who was he?' I said, 'Moses. Consider the trouble he had taking the Israelites out of Egypt and across the Red Sea, and forty years in the Wilderness.' That staggered him. I took no part in the debate, which failed to help the Government, despite the defence by Sir James Grigg, Secretary for War, and Sir Andrew Duncan, the Minister of Supply.

17

'Damn and Bless Him'

In 1964 the Labour Party met with moderate success. We won the election but with a bare majority, during divisions, usually about three. Harold Wilson, the Leader of the Party, had become Prime Minister and suggested I should be nominated for election as Chairman of the Parliamentary Labour Party; it was, he considered, unlikely that I would encounter any opposition, though I thought otherwise. In the event, my opinion was more accurate; I had not reached the stage of being popular with every member of the Party. Nor, indeed, have I ever sought to be. However, the election resulted in a convincing victory so I was duly installed as Chairman. It was by no means an easy assignment. There were acute divisions in the Party. We had, as usual, the divisive elements, the loyal Centre surrounded by Right and Left Wings. In the circumstances the Government was compelled to act with caution, much to the disappointment of the extreme Left Wing; but recalling the number of Socialist measures introduced and successfully carried through Parliament in the 1945–51 Attlee Government, it was now considered essential by the Government to give more attention to improvements in social welfare — pensions and housing — and seek to re-invigorate the somewhat sluggish industries which were not progressive in production, growth and modern development. I had two experienced colleagues, Herbert Bowden, now Lord Aylestone, Leader of the House, and Ted Short, now Lord Glenamara, as Chief Whip. For various reasons I insisted that the Leader of the House, being closely associated with Cabinet policy, should keep me regularly informed of Government intentions, which would at least help to avoid adverse reaction among the rank and file. The Cabinet agreed; otherwise instead of an occasional mild period of turbulence there would have been chaos. I learned to my surprise that some Ministers objected. It might, they argued, invest me with too much authority and weaken theirs.

Our precarious majority did not prevent some members of the Party expressing critical opinions on Government policy which were regarded as subversive or at least derogatory. My colleague, the Chief Whip, kept me informed about these members and their activities. They were asked to explain their critical attitude, but generally it was left for me to warn them. It was not long before I was accused of harsh discipline, even dictatorship, though in extenuation I explained that the lack of discipline, if permitted, would result in frequent defeats in the House. Nevertheless, criticism of my harsh style was eventually transformed into praise for maintaining discipline and preventing defeat. It was customary to have an annual election for officers of the Party, and at the 1966 election, though I was opposed by several MPs who sought this important post, I was able to hold the fort for almost three years. By the way, it was unpaid.

A movement was then initiated by the late Richard Crossman for liberalisation, which meant greater freedom for our members. In his opinion, this would promote harmony. An agreement was reached between myself, Crossman and John Silkin, who had become Chief Whip in place of Ted Short, to proceed along moderate lines, ending discipline. So we compromised, until it became clear that Crossman, now Leader of the House, spoke as if he was also Chairman of the Parliamentary Party. In my opinion — and my opinion was stated most forcibly — one Chairman was enough, so I advised the Prime Minister accordingly. Immediately he produced a memorandum and convened a meeting to discuss its contents. He was now in favour of liberalisation. It was a remarkable transformation. By this time we had, of course, substantially increased our majority, and Wilson's apprehensions of defeat were toned down. I was ready to compromise, except on one issue. As long as I was Chairman of the Party, elected democratically, I would brook no interference with my functions by Crossman or anybody but, if they wished, was quite ready to resign which, when I first suggested it to the Prime Minister, he described as a 'disaster'. It became clear to me that so far as Mr Crossman was concerned he would prefer the 'disaster' to my continued Chairmanship. So I politely, but firmly, during the discussion, handed the memorandum back to the Prime Minister with my resignation. I suspect this did not make him very unhappy. Since then the Party has never been free of trouble. Anyway, I was glad to resign.

Nobody loves a 'free for all' more than I do. To be independent, to do as one wishes, rejecting the views of other people — what a delightful existence! How happy we could be! As long as one does not expect a flood of beneficial results. On the record of facts, statistically and otherwise, changes imposed in 1968–9 affecting the behaviour of the Parliamentary Labour Party have made no contribution to the preservation of Parliamentary Democracy, nor has the prestige of the Labour Party in Parliament, in the opinion of the general public, been improved. Discipline, in principle, particularly of a harsh character, I reject, but just as I expect effective, firm and objective leadership from the MP who becomes Prime Minister, capable of a coherent sense of direction, ready to be unpopular if necessary, so I prefer similar qualities from the person elected democratically as Chairman of a Parliamentary Party, whether Labour, Conservative, Liberal or any other, without being bossed by a colleague who treats everybody as inferior. I therefore have no regrets, however unpopular I may seem to have become. I did my duty and sought to save the Party from becoming a shambles and presenting a spectacle of uncivilised behaviour.

My resignation from the Parliamentary Party created more interest than expected. It had not occurred to me that the Press, and even members of the public who are interested in the internal affairs of political parties, would regard my decision to resign as a significant event. I was mistaken when several photographers and Press reporters gathered outside my house in Hampstead Garden Suburb, focusing their cameras and demanding interviews; I had considerable difficulty in escaping, and on arrival at the House of Commons much the same interest was in evidence. Almost every newspaper invited my comments, some accompanied by financial offers that surprised me. At first I declined, because I had no wish to make heavy weather out of what seemed unimportant, though displeased at the attitude of Harold Wilson who said I had — to use his own language — prevented defeat of the Government but, now that we had a safe majority, was complacent about Crossman's intentions. So, with no desire to encourage divisions in the Party, when a certain Sunday paper with a substantial circulation offered payment for an article of only 800 words for a fee that had never come my way before, I yielded. The fee was really more than my article deserved.

Naturally there were divisions in the Party, some Members describing me as a harsh disciplinarian, a dictator; one MP, the late Lady Summerskill, for whom I had the highest respect, once called me a bully, while others applauded my wisdom because of firm handling of an awkward situation; it is essential when a government is in a minority. As for what was described as my courage in standing up to Crossman — if they only realised how easy that task was for me!

Among Press columnists who commented about the episode I mention Bill Connor, 'Cassandra', whose pen could so ably express forthright opinion of politicians. He wrote the following article in the *Daily Mirror* which portrays my behaviour accurately.

DAMN AND BLESS HIM

Sufficient time has now elapsed since last Thursday evening for consideration to be given to the conduct of the accused, plaintiff or defendant, the Rt. Hon. Emanuel Shinwell, P.C., M.P., at the weekly Parliamentary Labour Party meeting of which he is Chairman.

Dissident voice: 'What abaht Crossman? Manny can be accused of nothing and is about as plaintive as the Last Trump.'

It is further alleged that same Emanuel is guilty of being tetchy, testy, irritable, bad-tempered, irascible, petulant, hasty, touchy, choleric, churlish and captious.

Dissident voice: 'What abaht chucking in peevish, cantankerous, waspish and snappy as well?'

All right, include them in. Furthermore, the same Emanuel Shinwell is charged with being old beyond his years, aged and quite past it.

Dissident voice: 'What abaht venerable, mature, ripe and rich in his great granary of his years?'

163

Certainly, and we admit to liking your bit about the granary of the years.

Finally, we demand that this old dad, this Methuselah, this pantalooned greybeard, should give over and let youth have a chance and allow them as can run to join and win the race.

Chorus of dissident voices: 'What abaht using your commonsense, birdbrain? God help the Labour Party if it can't take a dust-up like this in the stride of its working-class clogs or its snazzy casuals made in Italy.

'There is only one charge that can effectively be laid against the Rt. Hon. Emanuel Shinwell. And this is that he permits people to call him "Manny" and even uses the miserable diminutive himself when Emanuel is the most splendid and euphonious of all masculine names, being derived from the Hebrew and meaning: "God is with us".'

Of course, Shinwell is combative, assertive, pugnacious and intolerant and we wouldn't have it otherwise. Damn and bless him.

When he first entered politics sixty-three years ago, Harold Wilson was minus twelve and Richard Crossman was minus three. Not one of the present full Cabinet Ministers, with the sole exception of the Lord High Chancellor, was born, and the vast majority were neither planned nor on the natal drawing-board. When Mr. Shinwell first became MP for Linlithgow in 1922, Mr. Healey was five and Mr. Crosland was four.

In the days of the Labour battles of the General Strike and the foibles of Ramsay MacDonald and the flowing furious eloquence of Maxton and the iron poverty of the Twenties, the more seasoned of the present Cabinet were shaking their rattles or bowling their hoops.

Age of itself is not a virtue, but the experience gained and learned from it by a mind still as bright as a glint of sunshine is.

Shinwell was and is rough and tough. Like Alan Breck in *Kidnapped*, he can ask himself: 'Am I no a bonny fighter?' and can reply with a thund'rous 'Yes.'

The man is of the gnarled roots of the Labour movement, and if the sturdy independent voice of the Back Benches gets hopping mad with some of the more intellectual Left Wing flowers that bloom in the Spring tra-la, well— so be it.

If Emanuel Shinwell must plead guilty to a charge, it is that of deeply and furiously loving his native land.

Following this high commendation from Cassandra, one of the most brilliant columnists in the newspaper world, but regrettably no longer with us, I recall attending a function in the North-East when the person presiding over the function, proposing a toast, made reference to Members of Parliament and others engaged in public life and said, 'Mr Shinwell, our guest, is one of the six honest politicians in our country', a remark which was received with loud applause from the assembled guests. When called upon to respond I asked a simple question, addressed to the Chairman, 'You have referred to me as one of the six honest politicians in our country. Would you be kind enough to tell me who are the other five?' I am still waiting for a reply.

It occurs to me that the article from Cassandra and other high commendations may appear too favourable. As a corrective I furnish a variety of epithets used by the Press media, some colleagues, political opponents and others which should not be concealed in case I should begin to fancy myself. Here they are: I have not the least doubt there are many others — 'arrogant', 'truculent', 'ruthless', 'Wild Man of the Clyde', 'fanatical agitator', 'firebrand', 'petulant', 'chip on shoulder', 'irascible', 'irrepressible', 'brawler', 'eats a meal of mashed nails every night'.

When Chairman of the Parliamentary Labour Party I was occasionally asked to suggest possible candidates for membership of the Government. That was no new experience because when Attlee was Prime Minister I was also frequently consulted, but I can never recall either when in the Attlee Government or as Chairman of the Parliamentary Party when Harold Wilson was Prime Minister, that any name I mentioned was regarded as suitable. In my experience over the years I have often wondered why Members of Parliament are appointed either to Cabinet or to junior rank who failed to possess the essential capabilities. Why some were appointed Heaven only knows, so here I make a brief pause in the personal narrative and refer to a somewhat exceptional intervention on the subject of 'shuffles' in Government by one of our famous English novelists, Charles Dickens. This is an extract from *Bleak House*:

CABINET SHUFFLE

There is my Lord Boodle, of considerable reputation with his Party, who has known what office is, and who tells Sir Leicester Dedlock with much gravity, after dinner, that he really does not see to what the present age is tending. A debate is not what a debate used to be; the House is not what the House used to be; even a Cabinet is not what it formerly was. He perceives with astonishment, that supposing the present Government to be overthrown, the limited choice of the Crown, in the formation of a new Ministry, would lie between Lord Coodle and Sir Thomas Doodle, supposing it to be impossible for the Duke of Foodle to act with Goodle, which may be assumed to be the case in consequence of the breach arising out of that affair with Hoodle. Then, giving the Home Department and the Leadership of the House of Commons to Joodle, the Exchequer to Koodle, the Colonies to Loodle, and the Foreign Office to Moodle, what are you to do with Noodle? You can't offer him the Presidency of the Council; that is reserved for Poodle. You can't put him in the Woods and Forests; that is hardly good enough for Quoodle. What follows? That the country is shipwrecked, lost, and gone to pieces (as is made minifest to the patriotism of Sir Leicester Dedlock), because you can't provide for Noodle. On the other hand, the Rt. Hon. William Buffy, MP, contends across the table with someone else that the shipwreck of the country — about which there is no doubt; it is only the manner of it that is in question — is attributable to Cuffy. If you had done with Cuffy what you ought to have done when he first came into Parliament, and had prevented him from going over to Duffy, you would have got him into an alliance with Fuffy, you would have had with you the weight attaching as a smart debater to Guffy, you would have brought to bear upon the elections the wealth of Huffy, you would have got in for three Counties, Juffy, Kuffy and Luffy, and you would have strengthened your administration by the official knowledge and the business habits of Muffy. All this, instead of being as you now are, dependent on the mere caprice of Puffy.

Dickens had, apparently, despite his repudiation of any political intentions in his writings, a rational understanding of those shuffling processes that are associated with British political life. Using different nomenclature he was not far wrong.

18

Travels and Turbulence

MPs seek to broaden their outlook and improve their knowledge of international affairs by taking advantage of the privilege available to Parliamentarians to travel overseas. Sometimes this is overdone, causing unnecessary absence and neglect of constituencies. Moreover, one has a suspicion that some MPs use the opportunity to enjoy an inexpensive holiday, the Government being responsible for most of the expenditure. My experiences of foreign travel, apart from occasional self-paid holidays, were limited, and seldom sought by me even as a Minister unless regarded as essential.

Since leaving the House of Commons I am not so well informed about those MPs who indulge in lecturing tours. Presumably some accept invitations and also seek them; they serve a dual purpose, a relief from the daily grind at Westminster and modest financial gain. Many reports followed those visits, some factual, others apocryphal. Two I recall. One may contain an element of truth. It was during the period when Ramsay MacDonald was Prime Minister, in 1929, and a Welsh Member, Rhys Davies, very eloquent and popular, made several visits to the United States. When about to address a meeting he was introduced by the Chairman, who mentioned that in England there was someone who was called Prime Minister, whatever that meant. The speaker was his right-hand man. On retiring to the anteroom after the meeting the MP said to the Chairman, 'You were very kind to mention my standing with our Prime Minister, but really I am not so important.' 'Don't worry,' said the Chairman, 'before you came nobody had ever heard of you; after you've gone everybody will forget you. Just sign on the dotted line.'

There is some doubt about the other story. The meeting

arranged was just about to start when the MP said, 'The meeting must be cancelled.' 'Why?' he was asked. 'I have trouble with my dentures; it will be impossible to speak.' 'Nonsense,' said the Chairman. 'Take them out so I can have a look at them.' Having done so he handed them back to the MP, and took out of his pocket another set. 'Try these', he said. The MP did so, but shook his head. 'No use. Sorry, cancel the meeting. I want no expenses.' The Chairman would have none of it, took them back and out of another pocket produced a set which he assured the MP would fit perfectly. My collegue played about with them, shook his head, said he would do his best, though he was sure to have some trouble. However, his speech passed off fairly well, and when about to sign for his fee expressed in warm terms his thanks to the Chairman. 'Without your help,' he said, 'I should never have managed. I suppose you're a dentist.' 'Not at all,' said the Chairman. 'I am the local undertaker.'

As a member of the United Kingdom Branch of the International Parliamentary Union I attended a Conference in Warsaw, the first time I had ever visited Poland. My active part in the Conference led to my appointment as rapporteur to summarise the general trend of discussions. During my visit I sought to discover where some of my ancestors had lived, but all I discovered was that my paternal grandfather was a flour miller who had lived in a small town in the Province of Kovno Guberniya.

I mention my visit to Poland because of an earlier incident in the House of Commons, which was somewhat embarrassing and may not be regarded as creditable. Speaking from the Front Opposition Bench, where I sat both as an ex-Minister and also as a member of the Parliamentary Committee — the so-called Shadow Cabinet — I addressed the House on the subject of Foreign Affairs. In the course of my speech I was suddenly interrupted by an Honourable Member sitting on the Government benches who yelled, 'Go back to Poland.' As I had never been in that country, and even though the observation seemed insulting, I paid no attention. (After all, I have probably made many remarks in Parliament that were not only un-Parliamentary but even offensive. Therefore I brushed the incident aside.) But a colleague, the late John McGovern, one of the Scottish Members, rose and asked Mr Speaker to demand an apology from the MP who had violated the traditions of the

House. Mr Speaker had no alternative and called on the offending MP to withdraw his remark, but he refused. My position was somewhat awkward. Without my colleague's intervention nothing further would have happened, but if I ignored the incident now that the Speaker had been asked to intervene, it might be considered that my attitude was cowardly — for me that would never do. So, on impulse, I left my seat, crossed the floor, walked up the gangway where the alleged offending Member sat, grasped him by the lapels of his jacket and tried to pull him down, but without avail. He just shrugged me off. Completely losing my temper I struck him on the side of his jaw, which seemed to hurt him. Feeling somewhat ashamed of myself I walked out of the Chamber, intending to take no further part in the debate. However, I was followed by one of my colleagues, who pleaded with me to return and apologise to Mr Speaker. In the circumstances I considered this was the appropriate action, so I returned to the House and made my apology, after which Mr Speaker called on the MP who initiated the trouble to respond, which he did, though somewhat reluctantly.

To my discomfiture I subsequently learned that I had inflicted some damage on his ear which had sent him for treatment to hospital, and it was suggested I should make a public explanation, expressing regret. I consulted one of my colleagues, a barrister, who advised me to take no further action. Then I made a more disturbing discovery; that the MP who was responsible for what was apparently intended to be an offensive observation was Commander Bower, at one time heavyweight champion of the Royal Navy. Had I known this I should never have gone near him, despite my occasional bursts of bad temper. As for the injury inflicted, it could be the effect of my punching the ball every morning before breakfast, a habit formed when I was rather more youthful and continued as a mild form of exercise. I was certain that Bower would retaliate, so kept a careful watch on him when walking through the corridors, but nothing occurred. Indeed, after making a speech about Colonial Development, which brought me some praise from colleagues and even a kindly remark from Sir Winston Churchill, I saw Bower in one of the corridors, but far from seeking to retaliate he came across and actually congratulated me on my speech. He has gone from us now; may he rest in peace.

This incident, widely reported not only in the United Kingdom but also abroad, was viewed in some quarters as associated with anti-semitism. That such exists in Parliamentary circles I have no reason to doubt, but in the incident in which Commander Bower was involved I reject any suggestion that he was animated by anti-semitism. It could possibly have been my interpretation of international affairs which conflicted with his opinions, or possibly my somewhat vigorous style of speech when making reference to the activities and threats of the Soviet Union. Yet, despite the existence in the three political parties of the organisation known as The Friends of Israel there are some Members of Parliament (many have departed from the scene) who, in both their speeches and activities, display hostility against the State of Israel and, incidentally, their dislike of Jews. I would appear to have been exempted, and have represented two constituencies — my first, West Lothian in Scotland — where to the best of my knowledge not a single Jew lived, yet I was returned as Member of Parliament for the constituency. In my constituency of Seaham Harbour, which eventually was transferred to Easington, there may be some Jewish traders or Jews concerned with some of the industries, but never at any time was there a whisper of anti-semitism. I have certainly had no reason to complain.

I must make it clear beyond doubt that, being born in the United Kingdom, my ancestors, whoever they were, do not weaken my allegiance to the country in which I was born. However, much as I dislike conflict among nations, my activities include effective measures to create a deterrent against conflict. I have a sense of pride in the State of Israel as an entity, but even more so in the courage of Israel to defend itself. This philosophy is embodied in my character. Whatever one may happen to believe, if one is convinced it is the right course then one must defend it with all one's strength.

Among the honours conferred upon me my role as Chairman of the House of Lords All-Party Defence Group is the most gratifying. Industrial growth and expansion in the future technological era, due regard to social implications and higher standard of living, are welcome, but equipment and manpower

— not for the purpose of conflict but as a deterrent against possible aggression — for defence is essential. If power and authority were vested in myself I would avoid war like the plague, and advocate universal disarmament, but in the world as it is, with nations whose policy is a threat to peace, who display the futility of international organisations to assert their authority and provide the deterrent against conflict, defence, however costly, is essential.

Throughout the years of this century strenuous efforts by men and women of distinction, undoubtedly with the most genuine convictions, have sought to promote universal disarmament. Unfortunately, as we know to our cost, their efforts have proved futile. There is no reason why their efforts should cease; equally there is no valid reason why nations should exempt themselves from the need for security based upon their relative strength.

In 1951 as Minister of Defence I was in New York along with the Foreign Secretary, Ernest Bevin, engaged in discussions with representatives from France and the United States — for France M. Schumann and Jules Moch, and for the United States General Marshall and Dean Acheson — on the subject of German rearmament and the removal of restrictions which were imposed on Germany after the war. I was staying at the Waldorf Astoria Hotel (not my choice), considered to be the most luxurious hotel in New York. Strangely enough, instead of enjoying it I was bored by the luxury food that was made available at every meal, and suggested one night to the major who was my aide-de-camp that we should ignore the usual dinner, go down to Times Square and walk through Broadway where possibly we could find some 'joint' and an ordinary inexpensive meal. We looked into the windows of some cafés and restaurants and decided to enter one of them. Sitting at a table we were approached by a waiter who, hearing what we wished to eat, said, 'Oh, you are English,' to which we replied in the affirmative and then, to our surprise, he asked, 'How is George Bernard Shaw?' Before leaving London we knew that Shaw was seriously ill, but to hear this question from this waiter in the kind of 'joint' we entered was really surprising.

I have had occasion frequently to visit Paris; indeed, even before the First World War, to attend many international conferences, and later, as a Minister, for negotiations with my opposite numbers. One morning when I arrived at the Ministry of Defence there was an urgent message from General Eisenhower, by then Supreme Commander in the European sphere at the Defence Headquarters in Paris, requesting me, with the utmost urgency, to see him. I had not the slightest idea what it was about, but arranged a military aircraft to take me over and arrived at SHAPE (Supreme Headquarters, Allied Powers, Europe). I met the General and some members of his staff and had some lunch — hardly up to my expectations of what one would be served in Paris. (I learned later that the General seldom ate more than a little salad; what the rest of us ate was hardly worth travelling for.) However, the lunch being over, Eisenhower asked me to go into his room and told me what the trouble was about. He was angry and I learned it was because, according to him, our Ambassador in Paris — Gladwyn Jebb (now Lord Gladwyn) — had complained about excessive expenditure incurred by the Commander's Headquarters. What form this took I never discovered. I expressed surprise to be called over to Paris for this purpose, which seemed to infuriate Eisenhower, who walked over to a corner and seized a golf club. He walked up and down, waving it round his head, and in language more suitable to the rank and file than from a General, expressed his opinion of the Ambassador and all and sundry in a fashion which, frankly, amazed me. I sought to mollify him, but it had no effect. To have to listen to this military expert, who subsequently became President of the United States, indulging in language which, having had long experience of Glasgow's docks, I could endure, was bad enough, but that he should also occupy my time in doing so I was not prepared to tolerate.

This reminds me of another incident in which the General was involved. When Supreme Commander of NATO he paid frequent visits to London. On one occasion he came to my office at the Defence Ministry when we discussed matters of mutual interest. The following day I had a message from the Prime Minister, Clem Attlee, inviting me to lunch where Eisenhower would be present. I went over to Downing Street, expecting one of those lunches where perhaps twenty people or so would be present. It was not so. I was taken to a room on the top floor — a tiny room — and the company consisted of the Prime Minister and Mrs Attlee, Ernest Bevin (the Foreign Secretary), General Eisenhower and, of course, myself. We had some lunch and then Mrs Attlee rose to leave. There was very little space in the room and I stood up and put my chair back to enable her to pass. Eisenhower also stood up. He was near the door and pushed his chair back and Mrs Attlee left. I pulled my chair back under me. Eisenhower, whether being absent-minded or for some other reason, failed to pull his chair under him and flopped down on the floor, looking up at me as if I was responsible and had committed an un-American action. I had not touched his chair. But the spectacle of the General lying on the floor is one I shall never forget.

After these incidents I came to the conclusion that though the General was a famous military expert, he was hardly the appropriate person to occupy the exalted position of President of the United States.

One of my most interesting visits abroad, on this occasion only to Ireland, was when I was appointed — as far back as 1920 — as the Fraternal Delegate to the Irish Trade Union Congress, held at Cork. It was during the period when there was turbulence in Southern Ireland, and the Black and Tans were in evidence. On the day of my arrival a number of people had gathered in a room on the first floor at the hotel where I stayed, and we could hear the rumble of military vehicles and occasional shooting. Then someone pushed open the door — he seemed to be a hotel porter — grasping a revolver. He rushed to a window, opened it and began to fire, at what we had no idea. Fortunately we managed to pull him back, closed the window and incurred no further disturbance for the rest of the evening.

The next day, Sunday, it was arranged that the principal members of the Irish Trade Union Executive should make a journey to Blarney Castle, and I was invited to join them. We had a charabanc and set off in the morning. Two or three miles after leaving Cork we were confronted by a number of Black and Tans, who ordered everybody out of the coach. The officer in command demanded the production of credentials. It appeared to me they were concerned about espionage. Every member of the Executive — all Irish, of course, and most of them local — produced their credentials. I was asked to produce mine. I had none to satisfy them, so they parted me from my Irish colleagues, placed me up against the wall, frisked me, discovered nothing more than a tin of tobacco, searched my bags, seemed dissatisfied and, for a while, it was uncertain what would follow. However, my Irish friends intervened and assured the Commander that I had come from Scotland to attend the Conference, and having, after some discussion, satisfied him I was allowed to return to the coach along with the others. We then proceeded to Blarney Castle where I kissed the Blarney Stone, which is believed to improve your oratory. Perhaps that is the reason why I have engaged in talking ever since! I had no sense of fear about what occurred: it just seemed very strange to me; but some weeks later I received a Press cutting of a report by Cathel O'Shannon, a well-known Irish journalist, in which he wrote about the event and asserted that the intention of the Black and Tans was to shoot me until he and some of his Irish friends had intervened.

One overseas visit I always recall with interest was in 1919. There were several reasons for travelling abroad that year, a succession of engagements. One was to Vienna where I was one of five delegates from the Independent Labour Party to the Conference of a newly created international organisation named the Vienna International. The Second International had been abandoned after the 1914 war. It was impossible to retain such an organisation when three of the member nations involved, Britain, France and Germany, were engaged in conflict. The Vienna organisation was described as the Two and a Half International, the purpose of which was to maintain during the war some semblance of unity among European Socialists. Two of the most prominent Socialist leaders in Europe were responsible, Otto Bauer and Fritz Adler, both intellectuals and engaged before hostilities as professors in Continental universities. These two men were regarded as the most capable of Socialist philosophers in Europe. I also met other prominent leaders, Grimm of Switzerland, Ledebour, leader of the Independent Socialists in Germany, and Jean Longuet, the grandson of Karl Marx. As a result of a speech I made during the Conference I was elected as the representative of Great Britain on the Executive, although I was the youngest of our five members, who included prominent British MPs like Dick

Wallhead, James Hudson and Roden Buxton. However, the organisation was itself disbanded on the termination of hostilities. Meanwhile, following the Russian Revolution of 1917 the Bolsheviks, having gained control, formed the Communist International and it was not until some time after the war that the Second International was revived.

The memory still fresh in my mind is what I witnessed in Vienna arising from inflation. The charge for eight days in one of the best hotels in Vienna was the equivalent of eight shillings and sixpence, and on my return journey, when I had been asked to address meetings in Munich and Nuremberg, I never paid more than half a crown a night in what were considered the best hotels. In Vienna there was grim poverty and actual starvation among the workers and even among middle-class families. Soup kitchens existed everywhere. I recall paying a visit to an institution where they were analysing soya beans to make them palatable for human consumption.

When I visited Nuremberg I was invited to the flat where a prominent German lived who had opposed his own country during the war. He was opposed to the Kaiser and was considered, now that the war was over, still as an enemy of Germany. I found him with hardly any food.

There is one pleasant memory amidst the gloom; a visit to the State Opera House in Vienna to listen to the wonderful music of Wagner's great opera *Die Meistersinger*, an experience I shall never forget. How often have I listened to the Prize Song of this opera, indeed, have used the record myself on more than one occasion when doing radio broadcasts for the BBC. In Vienna wonderful music combined with the utmost misery.

The purpose of those international organisations, starting with the Second International before the war — apart from the Communist variety — was to avert war. Regrettably they have failed, so did the League of Nations, nor does it appear as if the United Nations and the powerful Security Council are capable of promoting world peace.

19

Dissensions and Loyalties

While I was in the process of dictating these memoirs a momentous event in the political history of Great Britain was announced. A woman, Margaret Thatcher, has become Prime Minister, a more significant event in the year 1979 than the change of government from Labour to Tory. Yet few of the experts, economists, financial or otherwise, believed that the defeat of the Labour Government and the return of a Tory Government will solve our main problems.

The emancipation of women in the political life of Great Britain is in my long experience not a far cry from the turbulent activities of the Suffragettes before the First World War and the '20s and '30s. Now we have a woman Prime Minister. If this does not represent complete emancipation in the context of equality in the precise meaning of the term, it can at least be accepted as evidence of progress.

The new Prime Minister, whom I recall when we were both Members of the House of Commons, I would regard with respect as capable and friendly, but perhaps not as brilliant nor as outstanding as many other women Members of Parliament in the Commons or the Lords. I recall the famous Susan Lawrence, who could our-argue any Chancellor of the Exchequer, a model of language and clarity in matters of finance who could fill the House of Commons when she spoke; or Margaret Bondfield, able, industrious, well-informed, the first woman Member of a Labour Cabinet, and I also recall that most able and charming Conservative MP who later was elevated to the House of Lords as Baroness Tweedsmuir. It is possible to mention several other women Members, past and present, many of whom could rate favourably with many male MPs, but to select some and leave others out would make me more unpopular than ever. I have had sufficient Parliamentary experience to realise that to offend women MPs or the lady members of the House of Lords would be the last straw.

It is suggested, and apparently is acceptable by the general public, that the Labour Party is in a condition of possible disruption; that the Left Wing are gaining complete control and, should they succeed, future Labour policy will become even more extreme. Now, apart from the demand for more public ownership and the abolition of the House of Lords, there are apparently no original ideas, even some that might be accepted because of technological advance.

Let us be quite clear about it. The Labour Party, ever since its inception, has been repeatedly troubled by dissension. The items which cause dispute have varied from time to time. Acute differences have always existed. In 1900 when the Labour Representation Committee was formed, solely for the purpose of Parliamentary representation, and simply because of anti-trade union legislation, the leaders were at variance. In 1906, with the formation for the first time of the Parliamentary Labour Party, the leaders were more involved in rivalry about leadership than about policy. Some were suspicious of Keir Hardie, some of MacDonald; many of Snowden. Trade union leaders, like Tom Mann and Ben Tillett, were suspicious of the Parliamentarians. Indeed, for quite a long period, so was Ernie Bevin, who expressed contempt for leading politicians until he himself became a Minister of the Crown.

These differences, variants, disputations, disagreements, Right Wings, Left Wings and Centrists, should not concern us unduly. They are inevitable in a democratic — and what is believed to be a progressive — political party. A political party cannot remain static. It may take a step forward only to discover that retreat is essential. It may encounter obstacles in the path of progressive reform that were never anticipated. But in its objective of a civilised society, where the largest possible measure of contentment and security is attainable, where freedom of expression is not to be fought off but an indispensable quality in the system, where our resources — those of an internal character and those we possess in overseas countries — are wisely used, where distribution of our resources is reasonable and regarded as fair, based on a sense of justice, and when it is appreciated by those with sound judgement that those objectives are not attainable by slogans, well-worn platitudes and out-moded methods alone, such guiding stars may produce the form of society the founders of our Party envisaged. In seventy-seven years of membership I have endeavoured to be loyal to these basic principles.

I regard my transfer from the Ministry of Fuel and Power to the War Office as more significant than a minor Cabinet shuffle. It can only be interpreted in the context of loyalty among Cabinet colleagues. To assume, for example, that the members of the Attlee Cabinet, the first Government with a Labour majority, were in complete harmony either on policy or in personal relations is stretching the truth beyond limits. Reference has previously been made to the malice displayed by Dalton because he failed to be appointed Foreign Secretary, and to the attempt by Stafford Cripps to prevent the election of Attlee as Party Leader, and later to replace him by Ernie Bevin; also of the unaccountable but real dislike that Attlee had for Morrison. Attlee, as previously recorded, was himself the victim on three occasions of a conspiracy to have him replaced. In none of these conspiracies did I play any part, although well aware of what was happening. Moreover, Attlee, not long before his death, expressed himself as follows: 'Wilson is not a good judge of men. I would not give office to that clever fool Dick Crossman; no judgment, no commonsense, no judge of how to deal with men.' And as a demonstration of this loyalty — some might use the term hypocrisy — of one colleague towards another, I remember when Attlee bacame a member of the House of Lords and only then, in his second book of memoirs, referred to the so-called fuel crisis of 1947 and mentioned a letter which Stafford Cripps wrote to him in the following terms:

> I have become even more convinced that it is essential that a change should be made at the Ministry of Fuel and Power. I am sure this view is held almost universally by your colleagues, and certainly it is by the country and the industry in particular.

This, of course, refers to me, one of Cripps' colleagues! However, two weeks after the crisis occurred, which (as Lord Attlee said at a meeting which I attended, and has also written, all

179

borne out by Cabinet records which have been published after thirty years of my silence on the subject under the Official Secrets Act) was due to wartime neglect of our pits, shortage of manpower and excessive absenteeism by miners, and also serious weather conditions which were far worse than anything that had occurred for many years. Despite all this a letter marked 'Personal and Private' from the Board of Trade, Millbank SW1, and written on the day when the nationalisation of the mining industry legislation was implemented, was received by me, as follows:

My dear Manny,

I want you to know how much I sympathise with all your difficulties in the present critical time. You have had to bear the brunt of a situation that has come on us and I know how terribly anxious and worried you have been. I am sure that all your colleagues are anxious to help in every way they can and to share both the responsibility and the kicks. Good luck to you.

Stafford.

My late colleague, that brilliant advocate, was not singular in his views. I excuse Herbert Morrison because he was ill at the time. I would not have expected Ernest Bevin to come to my assistance or offer any encouragement as his correspondence with the Prime Minister about my intervention on the subject of oil indicates. Anyway, Ernie, big and able as he was, never liked anyone who failed to agree with him. Nye Bevan, when I approached him, preferred to remain neutral. The rest remained silent. In short, loyalty, or even — if one cares to use the term — compassion towards a colleague when confronted with difficulties not of his own making was seldom in evidence.

It is sometimes alleged that there are few friendships in Parliament. I do not suppose I made many. The fault would be entirely mine. There are occasions when one finds it impossible to agree with colleagues, even to co-operate. To do so without sincerity would be outright hypocrisy. I confess that occasionally I have refused to associate with colleagues, either in a group or a clique, or even on a committee. I have preferred to operate on my own. I mention an example.

When I was Financial Secretary to the War Office in the

Labour Government of 1929 I was asked by General George Milne, CIGS, to form a committee for the purpose of enquiring into the cost of maintaining and repairing Army vehicles, some used for combatant purposes and others for the Army Service Corps. Costs were increasing and expenditure had to be reduced. I agreed to undertake this commitment on the understanding that I should be the sole member, because of my reluctance to engage in long discussions with several people on this or any other subject. Naturally, I would consult all the available experts and make essential enquiries into every aspect of the problem. But to sit for weeks and argue with a number of people as to the appropriate action required, only to discover that even if we reached agreement there would be no guarantee of implementation, was something I was not prepared to do.

My first action was to consult two generals — one the Master General of the Ordnance and the other the Chief of the Army Service Corps. I did so for the purpose of gaining information, but discovered that they would hardly speak to each other and were deeply suspicious of my intentions, which might result in demotion for either of them. Consequently, I decided, without assistance, to visit the various depots concerned, and discovered that in the one under the control of the Army Ordnance Corps there was a vast number of vehicles; so many, in fact, that there was no room for any addition. When I visited the depot under the supervision of the Army Service Corps I found the place comparatively empty, and when I ventured to ask whether it was possible to use some of the accommodation for the purpose of accommodating many of the vehicles in the other depot I was told this was impossible.

After several visits to other depots I produced a White Paper entitled, 'The Report on the Repair and Maintenance of Army Vehicles'. This report was accepted by the CIGS and endorsed by the Army Council, and was a demonstration of how expeditiously and without too much argument it was possible to reach a conclusion.

Incidentally, I visited the Army Clothing Stores at Pimlico, closed on economy grounds, and, in going around, saw a vast number of bales packed on shelves which were marked with the date 1918, the year the First War came to an end. When I asked the officials who accompanied me what was contained in those bales they were unable to say, so I suggested the best way to find out was to bring them down and open them — the obvious way to make the discovery. We found the bales were full of wearing apparel in excellent condition, made during the First World War, but meanwhile at the War Office we were still asking for tenders for similar articles! This was another example of how to administer without the aid of committees.

I must not ignore an interesting and amusing episode which came to my knowledge during my period of office. Tom Shaw, previously one of the textile trade union leaders, was my Chief, the Secretary of State. He was inclined to be somewhat indolent and, indeed, remarked to some of my colleagues that he 'wore the feathers and Shinwell did the work'. One day I left the room to pay a visit to the toilet and there I saw a number of workmen engaged in knocking down part of the wall. When I returned to my office I buzzed for my Secretary and asked what all this reconstruction was about. He informed me the Secretary of State, who was a somewhat portly gentleman, found his occasional visits to that part of the building proved somewhat awkward and he required a place for himself. After which it was always described as 'Uncle Tom's Cabin'.

In the matter of friendship with colleagues, often there were disagreements, but that did not prevent me from offering assistance when any colleague required it. As an example of the reality of friendship I quote the example of my relationship with George Wigg, later Lord Wigg, which has frequently been observed. He became, as I have said, my PPS — unpaid — in 1945 at the Ministry of Fuel and Power, the year in which he first became a Member of Parliament. When I was transferred to the War Office he asked to continue the appointment, to which I agreed, and then when I was transferred to the Ministry of Defence he again continued as my PPS. Between us there have been many disagreements on policies, but whenever I have encountered difficulties during my various terms of office he has rendered the utmost help. On the other hand, when he sometimes had to face criticism for some alleged offence or un-Parliamentary behaviour, I stood by him and ignored the criticism. George Wigg, to my knowledge, did not indulge in alcoholic liquor, but I did and still do; he did not smoke and disliked it. I, on the contrary, continually smoke. He held views about the Middle East with which I violently disagreed, but the friendship remained; and what applied in this particular instance can be, in the Parliamentary arena, multiplied and even quadrupled.

There is one Parliamentary custom that does promote friendship, that of pairing. That is, a voluntary arrangement between MPs to absent themselves because of speaking or other engagements. One of my best friends when a Member of the Commons was the late Selwyn Lloyd. Our agreement to pair existed for several years until I joined the Lords, where the custom is not in use; Members of the House of Lords come and go as they please. When Selwyn Lloyd was Speaker of the House of Commons he usually had a reception when Parliament met at the beginning of the session. On one occasion when I went he was engaged in conversation with a lady whose name I knew neither then nor even now. He introduced me to her and remarked that he and I used to go to bed together. The lady was terribly shocked and was about to turn away when Selwyn said: 'Please don't worry. All we did was to agree to absent ourselves; he had a social function.' The term pairing obviously almost produced an erroneous connotation.

I have already told of my co-operation with the late Lord Winterton, one of the most right-wing Tories, an excellent but bitter debater who entered Parliament at the age of twenty-one. We became friends during the Second World War, when we collaborated in pressing for more vigour in the war effort, and continued on post-war reconstruction. A vicious opponent in public and so generous in private. Our co-operation was described by a witty journalist as 'Arsenic and Old Lace', the name of a popular play. I have often wondered who was the old lace?

I am not ashamed to confess that as the years pass I have — not deliberately, but through force of circumstances — become more objective. I no longer regard those who sit on the other side of the political fence as malicious, evil-minded; to be regarded as enemies. In short, one seeks to adopt an attitude towards colleagues of whatever Party and, despite contrary opinions, in a civilised fashion, and all the fancy airy-fairy talk about the virtues of democracy count for nothing if we fail to recognise the validity of my comments.

In criticism of various Conservative Governments during the period from 1951 to 1964 the Labour Party has described it as thirteen wasted years. This is a matter of opinion, but to those of us who sat in the House of Commons when Winston Churchill was returned in 1951 as Prime Minister, or when Anthony Eden occupied that office and Harold Macmillan and Alec Douglas-Home were Prime Ministers, and we in Opposition had bleak prospects of ever being again in office, for the years were passing and we would become too old to occupy office again, it was indeed a most distressing experience. It seemed at the time, during those thirteen years, that we were doomed to remain in Opposition, but what was the reason? It was because of the constant dissension that existed in the Labour Party, particularly on policy, but primarily on the matter of leadership. The Left quarrelled with those on the Right and a section of the Party Members occupying safe seats seemed to be indifferent. The fact is that after Clem Attlee retired seldom did we have either Party unity or effective leadership. The Party was divided into various sects — the Sherry set, the Hampstead set; and several others, cliques that were self-centred and self-opinionated, and invariably conspiring on the issue of leadership.

I confess that I fell foul of most of those people. Yet there were some who deserved the highest respect. I would single out, as one of the most worthy Parliamentary Members, Herbert Morrison, because of his vast services for the Labour Movement. Perhaps he was not a brilliant Foreign Secretary and ought never to have been appointed to that post, but he had the capacity for leadership. Moreover, the Party was torn to pieces by disputes over the nuclear issue, over German rearmament and security for the UK. One-third of the Party displayed the utmost indifference. In those circumstances, as I never had conceived the notion of being a Party Leader but was content to work with the Party whether in office or Opposition, I was not involved in any of the conspiracies. In short, I found it more desirable, both in the interests of the country and personally, to operate as an individual, sometimes objectively, but always with a concern about the national interest.

It occurs to me that I should mention an incident that followed the election of 1959. Following our failure at the election, which proved disappointing to the Party because of our expectations of victory, my colleague, George Wigg, suggested that I should approach Hugh Gaitskell, then the Leader of the Party, and offer my services in order to revive the spirit of our members in preparation for a subsequent election. Normally I would have rejected his suggestion, but was aware of the rumour that I was resentful because Gaitskell had become Minister of Fuel and Power, though not in the Cabinet, when I was transferred to the War Office. Of course there was not an iota of truth in that suggestion. We worked together at the Ministry on the most friendly terms, and when I left that Department he wrote me a most pleasant letter, expressing his regret because of the problems that the Ministry had encountered, and also mentioned that he would have preferred to have gone to some other Department. However, I went to see Gaitskell and we talked about what had happened during the previous election, in the course of which I congratulated him on his conduct during the campaign, but before leaving I mentioned that as I was an ex-Cabinet Minister and a Privy Councillor I might feel inclined to sit on the Opposition Front Bench, to which — to my astonishment — he demurred and expressed the opinion that some of the younger Members should have their opportunity to prove themselves on the Front Bench. Then he remarked that I 'could, of course, go to the House of . . .' and then stopped, but it was obvious what was in his mind. He meant the House of Lords. I confess this made me somewhat annoyed. The idea that after my long experience of the Party and numerous activities I should be put out to grass, and that the suggestion should come from somebody who entered the Party years after I had actually become a Minister, did not please me.

However, I decided to take my place on the Back Bench, not the Front Bench, and it may well be— I am quite ready to make the confession— that occasionally I may have indulged in some criticism, having the suggestion of the House of Lords photographed on my mind.

Incidents of this character, not considered important, can create wrong impressions and even lead to dissensions in a political Party. When we reach the point of no longer having respect for each other, irrespective of policy, then our behaviour and consideration for the other fellow have a more profound impact than loyalty to Party policy.

We must not always expect to be wiser than others. If there is disagreement on major policy it is open to members to resign. It is even permissible for a member of a Labour Cabinet or the National Executive of the Party either to resign, if in disagreement with the general line of policy, or to remain as a member and accept the situation.

On the question of re-election of Members of Parliament, no Member should consider that he is elected for life. There are certain risks involved when elected as Member of Parliament for a constituency. Sometimes it is difficult to follow the Party line or even the line adopted by members of a particular constituency. This leads to the only way open to a Member, that is to make a personal decision as, for example, I did in 1940 when many of our colleagues joined the Churchill Government and I refused. As I have made clear elsewhere, this was not criticism of the Churchill Government or an indication of opposition to the war effort, or disagreement with my colleagues. It was a personal decision.

20

The View from the Nineties

I have never regarded myself as an orator, in the same mould as Lloyd George, Churchill, Jimmy Maxton, Nye Bevan, Hugh Cecil, Derek Walker-Smith, and include Ramsay MacDonald during those formative years of the Labour Movement; there were many others. I have never been envious of those more comfortable than myself, but if envious at all it would be because of colleagues capable of making speeches regarded by me as more effective and better expressed. Frequently I have said — but only to myself — 'I would have liked to have made a speech like that.' I have certainly tried, but not always with the success I would have liked. I consider myself rather as a debater, in my element when facing an opponent, picking holes in his argument, even presenting the full text of the opposite case in order to reply, mostly deadly serious, sometimes I confess tongue in cheek, caustic, even injecting a touch of my special brand of humour.

Seldom have I used notes or even headlines; they bother me, so for many long years no notes were available. Often when asked about my method the answer is partly described in the interview I gave to Cicely Berry in her book *Your Voice* which every budding orator or those called upon to make a few remarks after lunch or dinner should read; and for anybody who wishes to adorn the theatrical profession. I told her:

HOW TO SPEAK AND WHEN

Sometimes I quite deliberately pause and appear to be searching for a word; I may know the word but keep them guessing, then out it comes. It is more interesting that way, gives them time to follow. It is sometimes said of my speeches that my pauses are more eloquent than the speech, because pauses are usually accompanied by gestures — a bit of drama. One of the difficulties about audiences is that, no matter how intelligent they may be, it is difficult to follow a consecutive speech, say one over half an hour's duration.

Sometimes, when I am looking down, people think I have got something written, but I have not. I remember an occasion in the House of Commons when debating from the front bench, Churchill was opposite me, and I was speaking eloquently — I mean consecutively, not in language that was superb — and Churchill rose to see what I was doing, but all I had was a sheet of notepaper with nothing on it! Churchill once said that it was an insult to an audience not to have something in writing — even his repartee was often prepared. I have nothing up my sleeve or concealed in a pocket. My critics say it is because I cannot read. Not true, I can.

What is important is to have a sense of humour, to be able to deploy it — I can do this. To give you an example: during an election I spoke at a meeting in Crawley — a huge audience — I looked at them and said, 'Have you ever heard of Napoleon Bonaparte?' They were all astonished — a remarkable opening gambit. I added, 'You must have heard of him, the Emperor of France, of course you have heard of him. You know what he did — he vanquished the Spaniards and destroyed the Dutch, and then thought he'd have a go at Russia, but the weather was too bad, so he returned. Then he declared: I am going to make of England an off-shore island of France — that is actually what he said — you can challenge me, just go and read it. But he failed — you know he failed — now it is left for Mr. Heath to do it.' There was much laughter; after that I could have said anything. This was during the Common Market controversy.

Another time, when there was much talk about the miners, I began: 'I see the miners want more money.' It was all about that subject so I asked a question: 'Anybody here doesn't want more money?' An extraordinary thing happened; one man put up his hand so everybody laughed. One must be able to do that kind of thing; it is useful if one is to capture the attention of an audience.

Having clear ideas is very important. I would go so far as to say that nobody has a right to address a public meeting unless the speaker's ideas on a particular subject are worth hearing. Also, many ideas are picked up in the course of a conversation and can be deployed when addressing an audience. Then there is the importance of enunciation; mine is not bad, I like to believe. You have to time it — no need to rush — one should speak carefully, quietly timing it, this is essential — and then you speak with passion which indicates sincerity— how one intensely feels about the subject.

I would go further and say that one ought never to speak at all unless there is sincerity and knowledge which justifies addressing an audience. You either believe what you say or you don't; if you do you convey sincerity.

In seventy-six years of my involvement in public affairs many significant events have emerged, both in the House of Commons and the House of Lords. One which deserves special reference is the election of Horace Maybray King as Speaker of the House of Commons. His ability and talent was fully recognised and, as Mr Speaker, when elected he gave Members of Parliament the utmost satisfaction. His election as Speaker was significant. It was the first occasion when a member of the Labour Party was elected to that exalted position. I had conferred upon me the honour of proposing him as our Speaker.

Two other significant events with public and personal reactions call for comment. One was Lloyd George's Coalition in 1918 when, having built up a national and international reputation, he destroyed it by forming a coalition with the Conservatives and some members of the Labour Party. In the event it proved a complete failure. Its achievements were negligible; its results disastrous. It stabilised an acute division in the Liberal Party which has never been rectified.

Another was the MacDonald Coalition of 1931 which need never have happened despite the American recession and the financial circumstances of our country. MacDonald could have remained Leader of the Opposition instead of almost wrecking the Labour Party. In the event his action achieved nothing of consequence either in social reform or economic and industrial development. In 1922, as already mentioned, ironical as it appears, I had proposed him as Leader of the Labour Party despite formidable opposition. In 1935 I contested the issue with him at the Seaham election and defeated him by an overwhelming majority. Nothing to boast about, it was my duty.

Coalitions in the United Kingdom, apart from wartime, are ineffective. We are too democratic for coalitions — we like to argue, to contend, to confront — in my judgement, except an occasional period of co-operation on matters of supreme national importance where consensus is essential — a course I have frequently advocated, both in the Commons and in the House of Lords. I have no objection to proportional representation, which would appear to be more democratic than the existing method of election, but with this reservation: not expressly for the purpose of alliance with another party and forming a coalition — if such could happen we must accept it — or enabling one party, however small in numbers, to hold the balance of power in Parliament. If proportional representation is acceptable to the electors and in operation, we must ensure that no vote of censure on a government should be accepted unless voted by 75 per cent of MPs representing all parties in the House of Commons.

The 'coalition' between the Labour Party and the trade unions is a special case. I have attended all but two or three of the Labour Party Annual Conferences since 1918, and before that I was a regular attender at the Annual Conferences of the Independent Labour Party. I have never regarded the Annual Conference of the Labour Party as any more than a 'get together' providing for the expression of views by those associated with the Labour Movement, either as trade union or individual members. Throughout the years the decisions taken at Conferences have been determined by the block vote of the trade unions, the largest numerical section of the Party, who provide the bulk of finance without which the Party could not exist. On the whole, despite the criticism levelled against the block vote, it is my view that the Party would have disintegrated long ago without it. It is doubtful whether we could ever have made progress without the trade union alliance. There is nothing objectionable about such a coalition, no more than the Tory Party's dependence on industrial and business interests. As for the question of Conference decisions providing the groundwork in manifestos preceding elections, or any aspect of policy, this is nonsensical. Conferences change annually, both in personnel and in policy. We must take note of what is said, what is advocated, what is decided, and decide on what we think is appropriate in the circumstances.

As I made clear in the first chapter of this book, it was not my intention to write a political memoir. I have contented myself so far as was practicable with incidents of personal involvement. This relates in particular to the deliberations of the Attlee Government, the full story of which has yet to be told.

In the context of Labour's ideological objective, it is doubtful if, apart from the Attlee Government of 1945–51, any Labour Government has proved an unqualified success. Even the government of Attlee, though favoured with a Parliamentary majority of 184 which pushed through Parliament at least 25 per cent of its declared programme, faded away deplorably in 1949 when forced to devalue and adopt the austerity policy of Stafford Cripps. The first two minority governments, 1924 and 1929–31 — I was a member of both, no use denying it — proved disastrous. The 1924 government was shattered by a political earthquake to which reference has already been made, namely the Campbell case and the subsequent Zinoviev letter. Moreover, progress was frequently checked by dissension, sometimes on policy and more often than not on personal rivalries. Even the support of the Trade Union Movement without which it is alleged — and with considerable truth — the Labour Party would hardly be able to survive, was conditional. Several trade union leaders were less than enthusiastic about the policies and Parliamentary activities of the political wing. Even Ernie Bevin when General Secretary of the Transport Workers' Union — perhaps the most influential trade union leader in Britain — was cynical about the politicians; he more than once expressed contempt for those politicians who believed they were more capable in Parliament of producing desirable beneficial reforms than the trade unions could secure by industrial action. True enough, when Bevin, in 1940 at the outbreak of the Second World War, became a Member of Parliament and Minister of Labour, the experience he gained undoubtedly changed his views on the subject.

Moreover, policy pursued by the political wing has not always proved acceptable to the industrial section as, for example, the controversy about collective bargaining or a statutory incomes policy. For myself I have never believed that in a civilised society envisaged by the Labour Movement wages and working conditions should always be determined by market forces; in short, that those who are strong in organisation or because of special skill or craftsmanship should gain the upper hand. In my view industrial policy, insofar as it concerns those who labour and render service, should be determined by negotiations concerning the individual interest of every worker, but must not disregard the national interest. I dispute the belief that collective bargaining since the beginning of this century has proved beneficial, either to the working classes or to our economic progress. Governments must not be precluded from intervention of the important subjects of wages and earnings. We constantly approach governments on other aspects of policy involving legislation. For example, the standard of living. Then why exclude wages and salaries?

As a member of the Attlee Government of 1945 following Cabinet discussion on the wages issue, I was challenged to produce a National Wages Policy, which I suggested was essential if we were to avoid industrial trouble. My Cabinet paper submitted in 1946, and now no longer secret, provided for the creation of an Economic Council thoroughly representative, assisted by experts fully seized of the importance of the subject, disregarding personal influence and focusing attention on productivity, differentials, the cost of living, the need for economic standards and a policy capable of providing security of employment and avoiding disastrous industrial disputes.

A majority in the Cabinet would have none of it. Nevertheless, I think it might be worth while to quote from this document.

> The traditional system of collective wage-bargaining conducted industry by industry has serious shortcomings under present-day economic conditions. A situation of general labour shortage naturally offers favourable opportunities for wage increases throughout the system. But in conditions of full employment, general increases in wage-rates may easily fail to secure any increase in the real income of wage-earners as a whole, since they will generally lead to price increases of at least similar dimensions. Moreover, in addition to failing in their objective of raising the standard of living of wage-earners as a whole, such general wage increases may . . . undermine the price stabilisation policy which lies at the basis of our whole economic planning. So long as wage-fixing is undertaken independently industry by industry (whether by collective bargaining, conciliation boards or any other methods) there can be no

guarantee that wages in general will not rise faster than is compatible with the requirements of a stable price level . . .

It is clear that although wage-earners as a whole cannot gain by excessive pushing up of money wage rates, this is not true of each individual wage-group. In a general scramble for wage increases carrying price increases in their wake, there is always a chance that the more powerful and better organised unions may secure wage increases in the industries for which they are responsible more rapidly and on a greater scale than those secured by the weaker or less well organised workers. Even though the real income accruing to wage-earners as a whole may not increase, the better organised workers may in this way be able to increase their share of it at the expense of their less fortunate fellows. Moreover, for every union that is actually in a position to improve the relative situation of its members in such a free-for-all wage scramble, there would be a number of others who would think they could do so — although, in fact, they might well lose. It is because of the genuine conflict of interest involved, that some judicial or executive authority is necessary to ensure a national wages policy consistent with the requirements of general economic planning. It is true that the acceptance of such an authority in place of the traditional system of unrestricted individual collective bargaining will call for a considerable effort of self-restraint and sense of working class solidarity, particularly on the part of the larger and more powerful unions. Yet this measure of self-restraint is absolutely essential if we are to secure any stability in our economic system in conditions of full employment, and in particular if we are to influence the flow of man-power into the industries and trades where it is most urgently needed.

Have conditions, social, industrial or otherwise, improved in my time? Trade union pressure combined with legislation has effected substantial improvements in living and social standards. Housing is still far from satisfactory; far too many are homeless, but the situation is nothing like I experienced early in the century. Even the substantial element of poverty that still exists is less severe than before the First World War, or the 1920s or even the 1930s. Those who, like myself, have over the years campaigned for social reforms in housing, employment and social conditions, and for a higher standard of living, are naturally far from satisfied. Neither trade union pressure, however powerful, nor Parliamentary activity has produced the security we sought, fairer distribution of wealth, or removed class divisions. Some workers have gained substantially; the miners, for example. Their conditions at the beginning of this century and for several years afterwards were deplorable and unworthy of a civilised society.

If it is our intention to abolish the Capitalist system or transform it, it is essential to have clear ideas about the alternative. What kind of society should replace the present system? Slogans like Equality; Participation; Improved Living Standards, etc., are insufficient. Plans in broad outline, with due regard to effective operation and consequences, are essential. I doubt whether every trade union leader advocating public ownership has a clear idea of how nationalisation should work and what are the responsibilities of producers and consumers. If plans have been prepared, the public are entitled to be informed. Even the policy of a mixed economy, which is now accepted as the policy of the Labour Party itself, needs clarification. I confess to being unhappy about the situation in the United Kingdom and in the world at large. How I wish I could find the solution, but if the experts to whom I have referred are baffled, how can I hope to meet with success?

I have engaged in many disputes and struggles. Some of the struggles have been self-inflicted owing to an excessive sense of independence. I have sought to create my own moral standards in public and private life according to my fashion. I have much, no doubt, to be sorry for — errors of judgement, problems caused by an irascible temper, sometimes out of control. I am never excessively confident about either my ability or my achievements. Yet I was often sure I was right, and in the event have been proved so.

In seeking to portray my character, behaviour and political convictions, I am conscious of omissions; many episodes, personal activities, though not ignored by me, may have been presented in somewhat superficial fashion. I have refrained from commenting on events where my knowledge is limited; it is unwise to be dogmatic or to commit myself exclusively to an established principle or belief. We live in a world of constant change. I express curiosity about the future, that is understandable. I have always wished to see what was on the other side of the hill. On those issues of theological concern, where for centuries controversy, violence, even persecution have harassed mankind, my tongue remains silent. In periods of meditation I have wondered about one's purpose in life. I read, I listen, engage in conversation, respect the sincerely held beliefs of others: nevertheless, I confess failure in reaching a conclusion. In this vast illimitable universe, so incomprehensible, all one can claim with limited mental apparatus is to reflect on the mystery of it all. To quote on those lines of the poet Keats:

— then on the shore
Of the wide world I stand alone, and think
Till love and fame to nothingness do sink.

To have survived the vicissitudes and strifes of a long life, frustrations, moments of desperation, even tragedy in the departure of loved ones, and even though in later periods of life one is accompanied by ailments, solitude and other penalties, one must be grateful. A long life has enabled one to widen experience, gain knowledge, the preface to understanding. That it is accompanied by periods of trauma when memory overcomes reason, I admit. So how do I live now, when in my ninety-sixth year? Until a few months ago I alternated between my typewriter and my kitchen. Now, apart from attendance at the House of Lords, a few functions — less now than ever — I am engaged in the dictation of a book, a task I was reluctant to undertake, and have only done so under pressure; more of a challenge than an adventure.

When the House of Lords terminates its proceedings some time in the evening, but not too late, I repair to my flat and, depending on the mood, devote myself as much to the kitchen as to the typewriter. Indeed, I confess that I often meet with disaster with both. Domestic help is minimal. I do not mind being alone and enjoy meditation about world problems; the past and people I have admired and loved, and gratitude for the services of experts in the medical profession; and when faced by periods of melancholy aware that one is better off than most; sometimes off-colour, but try hard to shake it off. If, when not in good form, I have to make a speech or ask a question in the Lords I feel much better. It is stimulating, even if one's speech is unacceptable or even ignored.

There is much for which one can be grateful. I have had the fortune to meet some of the finest, talented and greatest of men in the political sphere, in industry and many of the professions; gained their affection, even their admiration. Nor can I fail to recall the love of some of the most wonderful women. So I now take leave of my readers — with those immortal lines of the poet, Henley:

> Out of the night that covers me,
> Black as the Pit from pole to pole,
> I thank whatever gods may be
> For my unconquerable soul.
>
> In the full clutch of circumstance
> I have not winced nor cried aloud.
> Under the bludgeonings of chance
> My head is bloody, but unbowed.
>
> It matters not how strait the gate,
> How charged with punishments the scroll,
> I am the master of my fate:
> I am the captain of my soul.

INDEX

Note: throughout the index Manny Shinwell is referred to as E.S.